lyn peterson's
real life
decorating

CREATIVE HOMEOWNER®

lyn peterson's
real life
decorating

CREATIVE HOMEOWNER®, Upper Saddle River, New Jersey

CREATIVE HOMEOWNER PRESS®
A Division of Federal Marketing Corp.
Upper Saddle River, NJ

Editorial Director: Timothy O. Bakke
Art Director: W. David Houser
Production Manager: Stanley Podufalski

Senior Editor, Decorating Books: Kathie Robitz
Photo Editing: Lynn Elliott, Kathie Robitz
Photo Research: Amla Sanghvi, Stanley Sudol
Copy Editor: Ellie Sweeney
Editorial Assistant/Proofreader: Laura DeFerrari
Contributing Writer: Jill Kirchner

Book Designer: Monduane Harris
Illustrator: Janet Kroenke

Front Cover Type Treatment: Jan H. Greco
Front Cover Photography: George Ross

Back Cover Design: Monduane Harris
Back Cover Photography: Courtesy of Motif Designs; portrait by George Ross

Manufactured in the United States of America

Current Printing (last digit)
10 9 8 7 6 5 4 3

Lyn Peterson's Real Life Decorating, First Edition
Library of Congress Catalog Card Number: 00-103500
ISBN: 1-58011-028-2

CREATIVE HOMEOWNER PRESS®
A Division of Federal Marketing Corp.
24 Park Way
Upper Saddle River, NJ 07458
Web site: **www.creativehomeowner.com**

ACKNOWLEDGMENTS

THANKS, THANKS, and more THANKS

To my kids: Amer, Kris, Erik and PF. Thanks guys . . . for tolerating me. It's not easy living with certified OCDD (obsessive-compulsive decorating disorder). I am sure that sometimes you thought the house came first, but it didn't. I just wanted to make a home for you, a lure, a magnet that you would never want to leave. Judging by the frequency with which the front door opens and slams shut, I guess it worked.

To my sister, Chris, and my brother, Paul, for letting me come first (big sister); my sister-in-law, Paula Friberg, the picker for our many antiquing trips; and Carmen Loarca, the Guatemalan me, the glue who holds our family together.

To my sounding board at Motif Designs: BJ Sharpe for her photo editing; Maureen Rooney, JoAnn Breznicky, Fran Principe, and Kim Graham for all the great input and Michelle Sullivan for rounding up all the bits and pieces. To my friends: Kristiina Ratia for her good sense and great taste and Pat Farrell for the roses and the thorns.

Thanks to Jill Kirchner for her eloquence; Marita Thomas for additional help; my editor Kathie Robitz for her generosity and wisdom; Monduane Harris for her great graphics; Robert Grant and George Ross and Maryellen Stadtlander for their picture-perfect photos; Jackie Burton for her wit and charm; Chris Powell, architect, for the great bones of many of these projects and Mario Barbutto of MAS Construction for building them; Mr. Castro and Thayer; Al Haffid for hanging the paper; Anna for sewing the drapes, and Michael of Michael's Upholstery for covering the furniture. Special thanks to Creative Homeowner for launching my book program.

Thank you to all my wonderful clients who taught me over the years everything I didn't learn at my mother's knee or through a baptism by fire at home: Marcia Cohen and Estelle Horowitz for the best yet mother-daughter shopping; the Robertsons for buying my first house and for the music; Ann Lamont for oversize tubs; Eileen Coburn for the conversation; Judy & Allen Zern for friendship; Jim & Nancy Utaski for believing in me; Susan, Steve, and Matt (my other son) Becker; Bart and Sue (mini me) Blatt; the Ammiratis for attention to detail; Roni & Robert Lemle for our growing years; Cheri (& Harold) Kaplan for exquisite taste and generosity; Jessica and Lou Marinaccio and "the force" Leah Mullin for long-distance sharing and caring, good sentence structure, and a great finished product; Colleen Murphy for the color and the focus; Susan and Ralph Carlton for the pure fun of it; Mollie Schiff, 91, for "this is it" decorating; the Delehantys for planning and sticking to a budget, and thank-you notes from Adam; Judy "Bat Girl" Shaw for perfection; the Mullaneys for family; Susan Leventhal and Dana Calderwood for Saturdays; the Kearns for being my kind of people; JoAnn Jensen for word of mouth and being herself; Sara Bernstein for the shared teenager dramas; Christina Webers for her grace under pressure; the Whitneys for a perfect blend; Phyllis Huffman and her mother, Sally, and the boys; Katie Brown for the gardens; the Beckett/Giardini family for good skin and good shelters; Nancy Solomon for always having the right tool and the right solution; and Kathleen Hricik for being as good as me at decorating but thankfully for having a day job.

To my expert experts: Pia Mancini of Pia's Decorators; Paul Marcus of Manhattan Cabinetry; Joe Minovich of Computer Nerds; Paulette Gambacorta of Billotta Kitchens; Joshua Steele and Carl Del'Spina and Jeff Stone of Classic Sofa; Constance Apikos of ABC Carpet & Home; Kurt Baraud Audio Visuals; Georgine Nicolai from EJ Audi.

To the Uncle Bobs: My Uncle Bob, Bob White (RAW Designs@WebTV.net) of Roy White Inc, who grew up in the paint, wallpaper, and decorating business and was invaluable to me doing research and supplying anecdotes and his son, my children's Uncle Bob, who makes everything more fun.

To my dad for teaching me that you should be unhappy once, when you pay the bill, and not every time you use the product (how often did I have to relearn that?) and that there should be NO SURPRISES. And mom, posthumously, who showed me the beauty and love in having a wonderful home.

To my husband, Karl Friberg, for his brains, slim hips, and kindness. Not only does he get up and feed the children breakfast and make their lunches, but he oversees their homework—LUCKY ME!

CONTENTS

INTRODUCTION

Real Life Decorating is about being **stylish and sensible** at the same time. As a young wife and decorator, I bought countless decorating books. They contained **lots of pictures and styles**, but none of them were useful. Every season I would once again peruse the new generation of decorating books at the bookstore only to return them to the shelf. I could look at glossy photos in magazines; these books didn't address my real lifestyle. I wanted handsome solutions to **everyday decorating problems**. I needed information—both personally and professionally. I wasn't the only one to feel this way. As a decorator, over the years I have been **confronted with the same questions** from clients: How high should I hang the pendant over the table? How deep is the right bathtub? **How can I be sure** that I have chosen the right paint color? As a person with

A place for everything for everyone. This cheerful mud-room features a real-life storage solution for keeping everyday clutter at a minimum.

obsessive-compulsive decorating disorder (OCDD), I find the answers to these questions compelling. Sure, we all want to know how to arrange our bibelots and knick-knacks, but we also need the hard facts about important things, such as hardworking kitchen materials and easy-on-the-feet layouts; good-looking yet sturdy furniture; upholstery fabrics that can take the kind of abuse that only kids and pets can dish out; practical, affordable window treatments; family-friendly home-office equipment; and so forth. These are the things that affect the way we live in our homes, and we need to get serious about them unless we want to constantly make changes.

Compulsive redecorating wastes not only the financial assets of your family but also your time. Recently I read a magazine article about a woman who had repainted her dining room 11 times in eight years but was sure she "had it right this time." Sure, until the next trendy color comes along. There are many things to do with our lives other than redo and redo again. Why not get it right the first time (or at least the second time)? *Real Life Decorating* will help you do that.

Real Life Decorating will also be your reality check. You'll learn there are decorating guidelines, but it's perfectly fine to relax the rules. I used to get impatient with others in the family

for not doing his or her part around our home. My son would ask me to read to him, but I was busy arranging my accessories or restyling my Welsh dresser (pictured on the cover). The children said mom was "playing with her toys." When my first child was small, I owned the obligatory white canvas couch that was fashionable at the time. She wasn't permitted to eat, drink, or play near it. Now my sofa wears a hardy plaid fabric, and the kids wreak havoc on it. The plaid just absorbs and buries the spots and snags. It may not be up-to-the-minute, but it's practical. It permits me the time to read more to my kids and spend less time on decorating and maintenance.

Sturdy fabrics and furniture can take the use and abuse of daily living.

Finally, *Real Life Decorating* is an answer book. I hope you will refer to it regularly, just as you would your favorite cookbook. What are the ingredients for a happy family room? What is the recipe for a useful computer desk? How much pattern can you add without spoiling the mix? That's real life. You only have one. Enjoy it.

CHAPTER 1

BEGINNINGS

An ancient Chinese proverb says that the most difficult step of a 10,000-mile journey is the first one. This is often the case in **decorating**. We hesitate because we are paralyzed by fear. What if I make a mistake? What if I'm wrong? How can I know what I'll like next week or next month, let alone years from now? To find **your true preferences**, start by stripping off all the layers of external influence — the pictures you've seen in magazines, the ideas you've grown up with, the way friends decorate their homes — and address the basic question, who am I? If you **choose seating** pieces that comfortably fit your body type, for example, or colors that **consistently appeal** to you, how can you miss?

This chapter will explain how to get rid of the decorating baggage and make beautiful, practical choices that have **staying power**.

A good place to begin a decorating project is by looking at where you live and *how* you live. Examine the style of your house and the size of your budget, too.

WHERE DO I GO FROM HERE?

Too many people begin a decorating project without a clear objective about what it is they want to do and how they're going to achieve it. They simply start shopping without thinking about where or how they live. They buy a modern oversize chair that will never fit through the doorway of their modest older home, or they purchase a delicate inlaid table that won't stand up to the dog who chews, the children who wrestle, and the soda cans that perspire and leave rings on the finish.

> *"Look at your home's intrinsic style, and develop a realistic budget."*

There is no easier way to waste money or make mistakes than to start shopping without first having a cohesive long-term plan that assesses your basic needs, the way you live, and your enduring likes versus temporary fads. Contrary to what you might think, when it comes to decorating, reflection—and even a little daydreaming—are far more important than snap decisions or instant-gratification purchases. When my husband asks me what I'm thinking, I usually tell him I'm building sandcastles in my head. What I'm really doing is planning every conceiv-able renovation and purchase for our 90-year-old Colonial house. In fact, this is the way I put myself to sleep at night. Instead of counting sheep in my head, I start at the curb, cut to the driveway, and before I make it all the way through the house, I'm asleep!

The benefits of planning, thinking, and dreaming are considerable. Be honest about things such as: How much time does the family spend watching TV? How many times a week do you cook versus just reheat take-out food? What amount of time do you want to spend cleaning and maintaining? Forget your fantasy of an immaculate home, and be realistic. How often do you entertain? Will you *really* water the plants? Assess the furnishings that you already own and can keep or rein-vent. Look at your home's intrinsic style, and develop a realistic budget. The more you think these things through, the more likely your decorating efforts will work for who you are. A good place to begin with is an examination of what you already own.

Look In Your Closet

After a decade or two of buying clothes, chances are you know the colors that work for you. Is your closet filled with every blue from Chambray to Indigo, or understated neutrals, such as Vanilla and Travertine? What are the colors that always garner a compliment when you wear them? Think of decorating as

The colors and patterns you find in your closet are decorating clues for your home.

creating a wardrobe for your home. The colors you consistently gravitate toward in clothing are probably what your walls should be wearing as well, with one notable exception: black. Though flattering to the figure, black is less pleasing in the home, except on accessories. Besides, a color that looks good *on* you is often flattering *to* you when you're in a room that is painted that color. If you choose colors based solely on the latest fad—the lilac or gray you're seeing in every magazine—rather than your own preferences, not only will you tire of the shade once "the moment" is over, your rooms will look dated.

Find a Good Fit

Besides color to make you look and feel good in your home, consider your size. Are you tall or small? Long- or short-legged? What about other members of the household? My best friend is a former fashion model with mile-long legs, whereas I have short legs but a long torso. Her most comfortable chair and mine are vastly different. I like something that's low to the floor, while she prefers a high-seated wing chair. A low-slung couch would crush my friend's knees to her chin. If you're small, a high four-poster bed may mean you have to free-fall to get out of bed or use a stepstool to get into it. If your husband is a former fullback, then fragile, skimpy, and undersized should not be in your design vocabulary. If he is small-boned and thin, oversize furniture will make him look delicate—probably not what he had in mind. A 98-pound client of mine was determined to own an oversized tub—until I took her into the plumbing showroom and made her get into a large bathtub, whereupon I photographed her. Because her toes couldn't reach the end of the huge tub she coveted,

Less is more.
Choose furniture that fits you and is not just a response to the latest fad.

"Our lifestyles dictate the paths we must take: they point us in the right direction and help further define our journey."

she realized she wouldn't have even held herself above water. When she saw the pictures of herself looking positively Lilliputian, she opted for the standard size. The point is that if you don't give a nod to these kinds of physical realities, how can you expect to be happy or comfortable with the results?

LIFESTYLES OF THE REAL AND REGULAR

Besides your color preferences and your size, think about your habits and the way you live. Do you have four children and feel tethered to the kitchen day and night? Do you work 16 hours a day outside the home and then retreat directly to your bedroom with dinner on a tray? Do you tend to stretch out on the sofa rather than sit upright? Do you like to read? Surf the Internet? Exercise? (OK, you hate it, but you do it anyway.) Do you entertain frequently or almost never? Our lifestyles dictate the paths we must take: they point us in the right direction and help further define our journey.

Draw up a list of activities for each room. Some rooms may only be for show-and-tell — "look at me" rooms like that decorating dinosaur, the living room. Others, such as the family room and kitchen, are workhorses with activities multiplying exponentially. The family room activity list might include TV-watching, bill-paying, playing board games, doing needlework, reading, trip planning, catnapping, returning phone calls, and friendly get-togethers. This multitude of activities requires comfortable, accommodating furniture. If you like to work on your laptop or make class-parent phone calls while your husband is watching the "big game," a desk or a sofa table would be a practical acquisition. If you entertain a lot, ottomans (which can slip under a table when not in use) offer a versatile way to incorporate extra seating.

Maintenance: More or Less?

Also consider how much effort you are willing to put into housekeeping. Are you more inclined to take a minute to throw a duvet over the bed, like my husband and I do

> ## "... consider how much effort you are willing to put into housekeeping."

together, or would you rather lavish extra time and attention on carefully making the bed, neatly folding and tucking in each corner, and arranging all of the European squares, neck rolls, and boudoir pillows to perfection? Will you realistically launder white-canvas slipcovers every week or wipe down the stainless-steel refrigerator ten times a day? Do you like your books and magazines neatly organized on shelves or randomly piled on tables where you can thumb through them? Will you take the time to hang every coat in the closet, or is it better for you to be able to throw them over a peg rack? If you have pets or small children, try to be realistic: silk taffeta curtains or dark carpeting that shows every crumb and hair ball is not for you at this stage. Do you or your children have allergies or asthma? Then tile or wood floors will be preferable to carpets. Be realistic, and you'll never second-guess yourself again.

Past Possessions

Look at what you already own. Whether it's the quilt your great-grandmother made for her hope chest or the Indian bedspread from your college dorm room, don't be too quick to dismiss what you have for something new. These items are the records of our lives. All too often I have had clients say, "Nothing has to stay; everything can go." They want only the latest and the newest. I have been a decorator long enough to know that the newest anything is soon eclipsed by something newer. Unlike a sweater that can be buried in the bottom of a drawer, an awkward sofa can't be hidden in the back of your closet.

Ever wonder why most antiques aren't American? Besides the fact that America is a much newer country, we are also a much more mobile and *disposable* society. The average American moves eleven times in a lifetime; the average European, only three times. Frankly, it is often easier to leave it at the curb than take it along. Your parents may have scorned their grandparents' ornate Victorian furniture and trashed it all for Danish modern, but can you imagine Prince Charles getting rid of Queen Victoria's bed for something brand new? I recently read about a table worth 50¢ at the time of the owner's death that had just sold at auction for $3 million. From now on, I am going to save all of my 50¢ tables.

But Is It Really Worth Keeping? We recycle our soda cans, so why not our couches? As you take stock of your existing furniture, ask yourself, Is it of quality? Can it be successfully repaired, restored, or

A refurbished old cupboard has charm and sentimental value.

refurbished? If it was made to last in the first place, then it is worth fixing. My cousin wears my grandfather's camel-hair coat. The coat is more than 40 years old, and granddad has been gone 20 years. Needless to say, the coat is good quality. So if something is well made, keep it. Or if it has sentimental value, keep it. Or if it has graceful lines, beauty, whimsy, fond memories, keep it. Or if you can't afford a new one, keep it. You can always discard something, but once it's gone . . . .

What's Your Style?
The Tear-Sheet Test

How do you decide what it is you really like? What is the litmus test that will reveal your true core, your inner decorating being? One of the easiest, best ways I recommend to my clients is the tear-sheet test. Get out all of your decorating magazines or buy a wide selection of what's on the newsstand; then go through them and tear out anything that appeals to you. Once you've accumulated a sheaf of magazine pages, go through them again and spread them on a table. What consistencies do you see? When I recently looked through a friend's file of kitchen tear sheets, she was surprised to find that all of the kitchens had green walls and white cabinets. She didn't realize until then that she had wanted a green kitchen. Take notice of the silent teachings of the photographs: What is it in each room that appeals to you? A color? The shape of a piece of furniture? The floor-to-ceiling bookcases? While you're at it, it's worthwhile to note things you absolutely don't like as well.

This is also a good way for a husband and wife to find common decorating ground. Both can assemble their own tear-sheet

Color inspiration can come from a bowl of apples or the sand and sea.

collection; then go through and look for areas of overlap. Even a new-age modernist and a tried-and-true traditionalist might find they both like matte-silver finishes or dark wood furniture or the same taupe walls, so at least there's a starting point for a project. In addition, I find that the tear-sheet test can help to pinpoint someone's style far better than typical labels, such as "country" or "contemporary," which can be either too broad or too limiting in describing a person's style or taste. And working this way can steer you in the direction toward good home-furnishing stores, fabric resources, or a designer whose work you admire, as well. When it comes to design, a picture truly is worth a thousand words, and a photograph

can be the best way to communicate to a decorator, architect, contractor, salesperson, or seamstress exactly what you want.

The lesson is: get in the habit of tearing out details that catch your eye, or you're likely to forget them by the time you need them, and find yourself describing in a thousand ineffectual words the kind of valance, cabinet trim, or rug you want. (You may even be using the wrong words.) My husband says his evenings are punctuated by the sound of tearing paper. And my magazines are painfully thin when I pass them along.

TRENDS AND FADS

Design gurus and decorating magazines are always talking about the latest this and the newest that. But are you aware that there's a difference between trends, which are long-term directions of great significance, and up-to-the-minute fashions and fads that change with the breeze? Torn blue jeans are a fad. Blue jeans, of which millions are sold every year, are a trend. Trends empower our decorating selections, whereas fads burn themselves out in a blaze of marketing. They are all sizzle and no steak. If you want a home that's going to look good and feel good for a long time, decorate according to trends, not fads.

I admit that, along with most people, I am often tempted by fashion and fall prey to fads. Sometimes I like to have

Classic furnishings endure while trendy items fade fast.

Is it a *fad* or a *trend*?

fad	*trend*
Vessel sinks	Undermounted sinks
The unfitted kitchen	Furniture in the kitchen
Leather-bound area rugs	Tassels, fringe, and gimp
All white walls	Wall color
Long puddled drapes	French-pleated drapes
Sleigh beds	Upholstered headboards
Sisal rugs	Wool rugs
Foam-insert pillow forms	Pillows with trim and braid
Oversize ottomans (except as coffee tables)	Ottomans on wheels
Waterfall faucets	Gooseneck faucets
Streamlined rooms	Quietly cluttered rooms
High-maintenance interiors	Family-friendly interiors
Big, loose back cushions on sofas	Sofas with semiattached back cushions
Ready-made curtains	Custom curtains with finishing details
Oversize curtain rods	2-inch-diameter curtain rods
Ceramic tile	Stone tile
Too many small objects	Personal collections
Bed skirts	Side rails
Stainless steel in the kitchen	Stone countertops
Conspicuous consumption	Quality

the latest, newest, most chic thing. I see a house in a magazine done in a wonderful understated British Colonial style with dark woods and neutrals, and suddenly I hate my inherited mahogany, my mid-period fruit woods, and my early Irish and English pine. Other times, I feel like a battered consumer: no sooner do I think that this is "it," the one defining look, the magazines shift course and announce: "Look what's happening *now*." But increasingly I find that I don't want to be a slave to the latest style—because whatever that is will just change again in five years, or less. Being a fashion victim won't make me smarter, it certainly won't make me richer, and it won't free up my time. Besides, nothing bores me more than to open up several magazines and see virtually identical homes featured in each of them.

Looking Ahead

Separating the trends from the fads can be a tricky business sometimes. Is the penchant for silver metals in accessories and hardware a fad that will be out next month or a trend that will hold sway for a decade? This is one area where a good designer can help steer you in the right direction (although a bad designer may be as wrapped up in fads as any teenager). Look beyond the current catalogs to educate your eye about good-quality furnishings and fabrics. Visit museums (even modern museums) and antique stores and shows to gain a perspective on what lasts. And when in doubt, stick with the classics—especially when it

comes to the pieces that must last decades or a lifetime—a dining table, a sofa, an Oriental rug. Use fashion for disposable decorating items, which are fun and inexpensive to change, or for things that get used up or worn out quickly: accessories, candles, bed linens, accent pieces. Choose a classic sofa, but add a splash of the latest color or pattern with a throw or new pillow covers. Invest in a fine-wood dining table or even a farm table, but cover it with a brilliant tablecloth or an old sari when you want a change of mood. It is safe to say that if it came around once it will come around again. It is only with the newest of the new that we need be wary.

MULTIPLE-PERSONALITY DECORATING DISORDER

The other danger in furnishing by fad is that you end up with no true direction or consistent style: one room is French country, one room is mid-century modern, another

A good designer will guide you toward furnishings that will last a lifetime.

is traditional, or all the rooms are a jumble. Eventually your home looks like a decorator show house after all the decorators have left. This schizophrenic style results when you are too easily swayed by what you've seen in a magazine, at your friend's house, at the fabric store, or in a boutique — all too often fads. If you don't want your rooms to lack true direction and consistent style, take the time to study your own likes and dislikes. (See "The Tear-Sheet Test," previous page, for help.) Respect the architectural style of your house. If you have a contemporary home, don't try to add ornate 15-inch moldings; conversely, if you have an older home, don't strip out all the detail and put in track lighting. I recently visited a beautiful Mediterranean-style house in California with intricate iron grillwork and terra-cotta tiles. When I went inside, I felt like Alice must have felt when she fell through the looking glass. I had entered a teal and black modern interior. Where was I? There is only so much about your house you can — or should — change. Nor should you want to.

Realistic Standards

I have friends and neighbors who have no furniture. They live in expensive homes and have good taste, but taking that first step, making a commitment to a couch or a wallpaper or a color, intimidates them. They are afraid to make a mistake because they are looking for perfection. Just do it, as the sneaker folks say. Just begin and do the best you can. Live your life. Inhabit your home. Give yourself license to make a mistake. As the French put it: "La

perfection n'est pas de ce monde." (Perfection is not of this world). Are you perfect? Are your children? Why do we expect our homes to be?

I had an epiphany recently about the price of maintaining high standards. I went to a friend's house and was horrified to see that six weeks after her move, there were unpacked boxes in the dining room. When I asked her when she was going to finish unpacking, she sagely replied that she didn't know because when it came to a choice between reading to her child and unpacking her china, she would read to her child. Good thinking. I don't want my children to end up on the psychiatrist's couch because each time they asked for a ride, or a story, or help with their homework, I was busy deadheading the flowers, straightening up the family room, or shopping for the perfect carpet. Once I realized I couldn't meet my own standards, I lowered them, and we are all much happier.

Finally, buy what you respond to. Don't think about it, rationalize it, intellectualize it, or explain it. If you buy what you truly like, you will always like it — as opposed to buying what you think is in fashion but isn't really your taste. If you consistently express yourself as an individual, a fabric woven of your personality and life experiences emerges. As far as I'm concerned, the only failed interiors are the ones without soul and with no real connection to the people who live in them.

Add personal touches to bring your home to life.

CHAPTER 2

COLOR

No other decorating component has more power and **greater effect** at such little cost than color. It can fill a space and make tired old furnishings look fresh and new. Color can also **show off fine architectural details** or downplay a room's structural flaws. A particular color can **make a cold room cozy**, while another hue can **cool down a sunny cooker**. And color comes cheap, giving a **tremendous impact** for your decorating dollar: elbow grease, supplies, prep work, and paint will all cost pretty much the same if you choose a **gorgeous hue** over plain white. But finding the color — **the right color** — isn't easy. As a decorator, I can tell you that it is tedious, anxiety-ridden, and yet the **most rewarding** part of my job.

In this seaside home, I recommended colors that are soft and inviting yet strong enough to hold their own against the strong coastal sunlight. The overall scheme had to be more sophisticated than typical beach homes because the owners live here year-round.

Warm neutral-color walls and touches of red make this bedroom cozy.

Recently, I had to choose a paint stain for a client's porch floor. Once the stain was applied, it looked nothing like the sample on the color chart and was clearly wrong—dreary and dull. I considered several alternatives and thought about them half the night. At dawn, I got into the car and drove around the neighborhood to check out countless other porch floors. When I arrived at my client's home at 8 A.M., I made a clear and correct new color choice. The process wasn't simple, but was it worth it? Definitely.

OK, you say, the right color is worth the trial and effort it takes to find it, but where do you begin to look? Like the economy, color has leading indicators. You have a market basket full of choices, and there are lots of signposts to direct you where to go.

THE LAY OF THE LAND

For the past 200 years, white has been the most popular choice for American home exteriors. And it still is, followed by tan, brown, and beige. You can play it safe and follow the leader. But you should also think about the architecture of your house and where you live when you're considering exterior color. For example, traditional Colonials have a color-combination range of about two that look appropriate: white with black or green shutters and gray with white trim. Mediterranean-style houses typically pick up the colors of terra-cotta and the tile that are indigenous to the regions that developed the architecture—France, Italy, and Spain. A ranch-style house shouldn't be overdone—it is, after all, usually a modest structure. On the other hand, I think a cottage can be fanciful but not daring—unlike the houses in Miami's South Beach. Even there, softer, more livable bright hues are replacing the early outrageous colors of the Art Deco revival movement. Whimsical colors look charming on Victorian houses in San Francisco, too, but they would be out of place in conservative Scarsdale, New York, where you must check with the local building board when you want to change the exterior color of your house. That regulation came into effect after someone decide to paint a prominent house in town electric blue. Which points out the need to reference your immediate neighbors' houses when choosing an exterior color.

I picked Louisberg Green for my clients, the Mullaneys, because all of the surrounding homes are beige, yellow, or

"Whimsical colors look charming on Victorian houses in San Francisco, but they would be out of place in conservative Scarsdale, New York . . ."

White-painted trim and molding stands out against color.

How's the Weather?

Like exteriors, interiors often take their color cues from their environs and local traditions. In the rainy and often chilly Pacific Northwest, cozy blanket plaids in strong reds and black abound. In the hot-and-arid climate of the West, indigo or brown ticking-stripes and faded denim look appropriately casual and cool. Subtle grays and neutrals, reflecting steel, limestone, and cement, look apropos for sophisticated city life.

In very warm southern climates, the brilliant sun bleaches out color. That explains the popularity of strong hues in tropical, sun-drenched locales. Think of the saturated colors of Provence — Sunflower Yellow, Grape Hyacinth, Azure Blue, and Poppy Red. Imagine the calypso pinks and oranges and the tangy greens and blues of the Caribbean Islands. Neutrals and whites work well in these hot spots, too, because they don't compete with the sun. They're cool, quiet, and tranquil, and they remind me of the crisp white linen worn on safari.

off-white. The color looks wonderful. Once the Louisberg Green was up, I settled on Indian Red for the deck. It looks great next to the warm tones in the stone foundation. In addition to considering the main color of the house, always look at the parts of the house that will not be painted — the foundation, in this case — and think about the elements that will receive a secondary or accent color. Paint the largest surface first (the siding); then review various choices for the smaller elements, such as the trim, the doors, and the shutters. The overall process is a lot like shopping for clothes: first you buy the suit, and then you pick out the shoes and accessories.

Natural Light. That's the one you don't pay for. Its direction and intensity greatly affects color. A room with a window that faces trees will look markedly different in summer, when warm white sunlight is filtered through the leaves, than in winter, when the trees are bare and the color of natural light takes on a cool blue cast. Time of day affects color, too. Yellow walls that are pleasant and cheerful in the early morning can be stifling and blinding

 *yellow*

YELLOW illuminates the colors it surrounds. It warms rooms that receive northern light but can be too bright in a sunny room. It's best for daytime rooms, not bedrooms. It has a short range, which means as white is added to yellow, it disappears. Yellow highlights and calls attention to features—think of bright taxicabs.

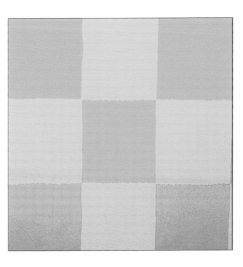

 *red*

RED is powerful, dramatic, motivating. Red is also hospitable, and it stimulates the appetite, which makes it a favorite choice for dining rooms. Some studies have indicated that a red room actually makes people feel warmer.

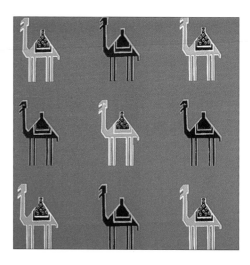

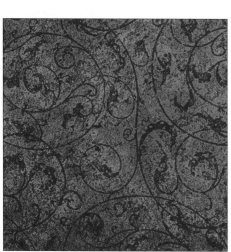

in the afternoon. That's because afternoon sun is stronger than morning sun.

When you're choosing a color for an interior, always view it at different times of day, but especially during the hours in which you will inhabit the room. It is inconsequential to me how my bedroom looks at noon—I never sleep that late. The living room is also more often a room of nighttime use. But in the kitchen, I want something that looks good in the morning and at the end of the day when I'm putting dinner together. In the dining room, color that seems wonderful during the day mustn't fall flat at night when I adjust the dimmer switch and light the candles.

Artificial Light. Because artificial light affects color rendition as much as natural light, don't judge a color in the typically chilly fluorescence of a hardware store. The very same color chip will look completely different when you bring it home. Most *fluorescent light* is bluish and distorts colors. It depresses red and exaggerates green, for example. A romantic faded rose on your dining room walls will just wash out in the kitchen if your use a fluorescent light there. That's why it's so important to test out a paint color in your own home, with and without the lights turned on. In general, *incandescent light,* the type produced by the standard bulbs you probably use in your chandelier and in most of your home's light fixtures, is warm, but slightly yellow. *Halogen*

light, which comes from another newer type of incandescent bulb, is white and the closest to natural sunlight. Of all three types of bulbs, halogen is truest when it comes to rendering color.

All This Means Is That Color Is Relative

I was working on a seaside house in Maine, and the color chip I picked out in New York that looked merely creamy suddenly read mustard-gold against the ocean view and the New England sky. The way a color appears depends a lot on circumstance—besides the natural and artificial light, the other colors in the room on the sofa, in the

Green-painted wicker brings a garden feeling inside this room.

I even look at book bindings when coordinating a room's colors.

pillows, or in the rug can all influence your perception. Even colors in adjacent spaces — indoors and outdoors — can affect each other. That's why the beige in your foyer seems perfectly lovely until you look down the hall into your blue kitchen. Suddenly it becomes an icky yellow. Blue, that dominant fellow, washes over beige.

The brain never sees one color at a time — except, perhaps, when you're looking at a paint chip. Colors are always seen in relationship to each other. (See the color wheel on page 55.) When you're looking at a color for the walls, look at the wood floors, the curtains, the view outside the window, even the book-bindings — all of them will sway your perception of the wall color. *Always view a paint chip in concert with the other elements.* Otherwise, picking out a color is like trying to isolate an ingredient in a finished recipe — you can't.

Optical Illusions. Did you know that your eyes retain an image for a full second after it disappears? That means the color of the room you just left is superimposed on the next room you enter, albeit momentarily. Other optical illusions can throw off your color perception as well. The exact same color viewed against another background will look different. Put red next to coral, and it appears maroon; put red next to purple, and it looks almost orange. On the other hand, when two colors of the same value (the

degree of lightness or darkness of a color) are put next to each other, they can disappear into one another. This is called *spreading*. I once designed a wallpaper pattern that featured a little light blue house with a light green door. When the wallpaper was hung, I was shocked — someone at the printer had forgotten to make the door a separate color! Then I looked closer and saw that I was wrong — the green door simply "disappeared" into the body of the blue house. This can happen when you put two neutral colors side by side, as well.

Confused? Overwhelmed? Don't be. Once you become aware of how color works, the process of picking the right one isn't complex.

IN SYNC

Don't even think about choosing colors if your furniture is in storage, in transit, or shrouded in drop cloths. Recently I selected a chair fabric, and now that the upholstery is done, the client and I aren't 100 percent pleased with the final result. Why? When I chose the color for the fabric, the curtains and rugs were out for cleaning, and the walls were white. Since then, the walls have been painted coral, and the curtains and rugs are back in place. Although the chair looks good, it could have looked incredible (and with a decorator, you deserve incredible), if I had waited until the other elements were in the room. We're redoing the chair now.

> *"While paint colors are almost infinite, the color for everything else is more limited."*

NARROWING DOWN YOUR CHOICES

There really are no bad colors—only bad combinations of colors. If you're painting more than one room, try to build a cooperative *community of colors*. Rooms on the same floor or within the same house should be good neighbors. A warm gold in the entrance hall may look sickly when the front door is open and the color is viewed alongside the cool gray exterior shingles. This doesn't mean that everything has to match, but when colors flow easily from one to another, they can lead the eye through the house and create an overall sense of order. Within a home there may be several communities of colors. Perhaps one comprises the living room, dining room, and entryway; the kitchen and family room another; and the upstairs bedrooms and hall a third (depending on the strength of your children's personalities and rooms).

Start with Your Givens. Many novices begin decorating projects by picking out paint color first, when that's what they should choose last. You don't want to paint the walls and then realize that you can't find furnishings or accessories to go with the color. In the living room, first consider the sofa fabric, the curtains, the colors in the rug, even the coffee table finish. In the dining room, the colors that will work best will be dictated, in large part, by your

china (unless you have a simple white service or are willing to start over). I recently re-wallpapered my bedroom. I love the wallpaper, but I have purchased and returned four sets of bedding—me, the professional. Finally, four tries later, I *think* I've found the right one. While paint colors are almost infinite—there are literally thousands of choices available in ready-mixed shades alone—the color for everything else is more limited. For every ten patterned rugs or ten ready-made bedding options on the market, there are about a hundred times as many fabric choices and a thousand paint choices. So, make your job easier—pick out your wall color last.

There Are No "Perfect" Matches

Too often I have customers who run over with their china pattern and curtain tieback and say, "Look, the yellows aren't the same!" They don't match because there are no perfect matches. What looks one way one moment, looks totally different when you turn on the table lamp, anyway. So rather than trying to match the wall color to a leaf in a fabric swatch, pick a green that "reads" well overall—do a lot of squinting to evaluate it from a distance. I find that if I close one eye and hold out my hand to mask out what I don't want to see, I can actually gauge color pretty accurately. (I have a lot of

An exuberant color scheme can even brighten dark nooks under the stairs.

Natural light greatly affects color rendition.

A color has to be viewed in isolation, first, and then with the other elements and colors in the room.

For each color test, do a "walk-by" viewing. After taping all the chips to the white background, look at them quickly as you walk by. Don't think, just react, respond, and see. You'll be able to eliminate many of the colors right away (except for some neutrals, which are harder to distinguish from one another). When you get to the final few, hold them in your hand, and move around the room, squinting and looking at them against various surfaces. Check them on north- and south-facing walls and on horizontal and vertical surfaces.

Color by Trial. Lastly, buy a quart of each of the finalists and try them out one at a time on a large swatch of one wall, preferably painted into a corner. This can get expensive, so try to be discriminating. Keep in mind that a color seems to get darker when there's more of it to see and, when all four walls are finally painted, the result will look darker than the trial swatch. Factor this into your decision; you may want to go a shade lighter. However, you can lighten any color with white, something that's much easier to do than making a color darker. So if you're in doubt, choose the slightly deeper shade, and then dribble in "ceiling white" or another white paint until you get the color that you want. Then take your sample to the paint store.

squint lines around my eyes.) But it's important to test out your choices, too. I tell my clients that choosing a paint color is a lot like shopping for a dress: no matter how good it looks in the catalog, it will not look the same on your hips or in your house. You have to try it on before you buy it.

First, take a fistful of color chips from the paint store home with you. Tape them up onto a white wall or onto a large piece of white poster board. (Don't do this with a colored background, which can muddy your perception.)

 *blue*

BLUE, with its associations of sea and sky, offers serenity, which is why it is a favorite in bedrooms. Studies have shown that people think better in blue rooms. Perhaps that explains the popularity of the navy blue suit. Cooler blues show this color's melancholy side, however.

The Big White Lie

It's a good idea to keep the items that you aren't going to replace for a long time neutral—window treatments, bath tiles, kitchen counters. Save stronger colors and patterns for easily changed accents such as pillows, throws, dishes, or towels. But if you're ready to throw in the color chips for an all-neutral scheme, there are a few things you should know. All-white rooms, though the darling of decorating magazines, are actually hard on the eye, not to mention almost impossible to maintain.

I call this decorating choice the big white lie because people who live with it lie. One noted white aficionado I know has a Hunter Green family room. Another drapes matelassé quilts over her sofas. A third keeps multiple sets of slipcovers on hand, has had her upholstery recovered twice in three years, and makes her housekeeper wash and redo pillow covers weekly. "It's easy," she says. For whom? In my last house, the kitchen floors were white. We mopped them daily and sometimes twice daily on weekends. In the new house, I decided I was not going to spend that much of my time on this planet maintaining white floors. Now the kitchen floor is terra-cotta. My philosophy? White is not a good investment—not in clothes, shoes, or interiors. It's just too high maintenance.

Shades of navy
relieve the starkness
of this otherwise
all-white room.

White is OK, but only for rooms that you can scrub down thoroughly and often (the bathroom and the kitchen) or for bed linens. Life is stressful enough. Why make cleaning up after it more complicated?

The Other Neutral

It used to be called "beige," and like all things that go in and out of style, that name is now passé. But like a good pair of khaki-colored pants, this neutral is a classic. Call it whatever you will—Sand, Seagrass, Toast, Tea, Café, Sepia, Ecru, Cream, Umber, Hazel, Topaz, or Tawny. Today's beiges are a bit more robust than former incarnations. We're definitely taking our Café double these days. As a decorator, I know the essential usefulness of beige. From the practical standpoint, beige won't show dirt

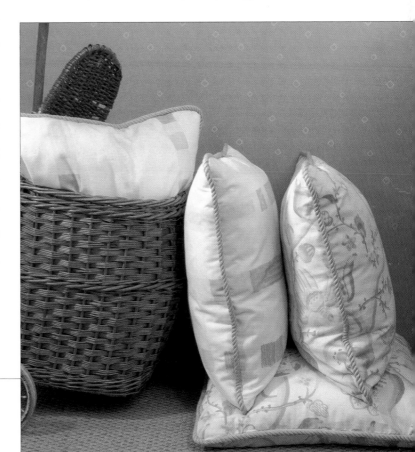

**Texture and
pattern** are good
ways to liven up a
pale scheme.

nearly as quickly as white. It's also the color of most stone and marble, and sisal and sea grass rugs—things that last. Use beige as a great platform for other colors. Like your khakis, it goes well with everything from Brick Red to Moss Green to Navy Blue.

Establish A Pecking Order

Every room should have one dominant color. Additional colors can be used to accent or play down certain features. When you're wearing black, one red accessory—a red belt, a red jacket, or red shoes—looks great. Wear all three red accessories with your black sweater and slacks, and you might look like a clown. Similarly, equal doses of two or more colors in a room can look like a patchwork quilt—very fragmented. And what happens when two colors of the same value are put next to each other? They spread and lose their sharpness, or merge and become one less-attractive hue.

Play Up Color Contrasts. You may be crazy about the color you've chosen for the walls, but if the room has beautiful moldings, window and door trim, or columns, painting them the same color is criminal. Draw attention to them with a contrasting color. I have an elegant old Palladian-style window on my stair landing. The beautiful wood trim around the window is off-white. For eight years the hall wallpaper has been one with a creamy white background and a thin Moss stripe. This year I reversed the look, choosing a paper with a Mossy background. All

of a sudden, the window stands out and assumes importance. Before it blended into the walls; now it is the star feature, and deservedly so. So whether you want to show off a window, a fireplace, French doors, or some other handsome architectural feature, use a contrasting color. Another way to do this is with advancing colors (bright colors or warm hues, such as yellow or pink).

Leonardo da Vinci was the first on record to observe that colors seen in shadow become more alike. Our color sensors simply don't fire in low light, and it becomes harder to differentiate shades. I learned this lesson the hard way on one of my first decorating jobs. I chose a cream-and-white wallpaper to lighten up a dark hallway. When I arrived to check on the results, I thought the wallpaper wasn't up yet. It was—but there wasn't enough of a contrast between the color of the wallpaper and the wall trim and moldings. The difference between them barely registered. I learned. In dark spaces, use a strong wall color against white trim.

Reverse Psychology. By the same token, you can also make elements that are in poor condition or features that you don't like seem to disappear by painting them out. For example, if you want to play down large sliding closet doors or windows that are asymmetrical or oddly placed, paint them the same color as the walls. Another way to do this is with receding colors (dark hues or cool colors, such as blue or green).

 *purple*

PURPLE is royal, independent. True purple is a mixture of equal amounts of red and blue. Various shades of the color range from deep eggplant to delicate lavender. As a decorating color, it goes in and out of fashion but always looks pretty as a pastel or as an accent.

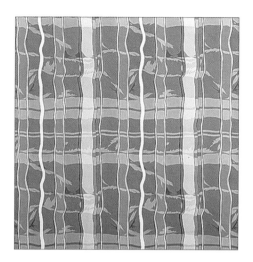

Accent Walls. I usually don't go for an accent wall because it can make a typical four-sided room feel as though it stops short. However, there are situations that can use an accent wall to advantage. For example, great rooms with high ceilings can often feel large and empty. Treating the far wall (usually the fireplace wall) as an accent wall can be a powerful and effective way to "fill up" the room using color. In a playroom without lots of furniture and fabrics, a contrasting wall can be, well, playful and fun. In a room with an alcove or window bay, a second color can emphasize a sense of separation and make the niche seem larger and more special. In a playroom I decorated, neutral gray made a clean, contemporary backdrop for all the toys and electronics, but it was a little cold. All red would have been too much, so I painted just the window

COLOR

Color always appears darker on the ceiling and beams in a room because horizontal planes don't reflect as much light as vertical planes (walls). I almost always paint ceilings a cheap, very light flat-finish called "ceiling white." But, recently, a client of mine insisted on painting her ceiling, which had a boxed-pipe overhang, the same Dove White that we chose for the walls. When it was done, she was sure the ceiling paint was a darker color. Of course, it wasn't—the appearance of the color changed as it moved from horizontal to vertical plane.

"if you always gravitate to one or two colors, stick with them."

bay (including its dropped ceiling) Brick Red, and it looks great. Another use for an accent color can be to define space. If one end of a room has a separate function, such as a sort of hallway or dining area, a contrasting color can create the effect of a separate room.

Be True To Yourself

A few years ago, I decided I had enough of my signature Moss and Rose, so I decorated my screened porch in blue. (It's really my sister's color scheme, but I like it, too.) What a mistake! Now when I step onto the porch, I feel as if I have multiple personality decorating disorder—it's not me, not to mention the fact that when I bring out my Camel throw, green stemware, or red transferware, they look all wrong and out of place. Even my napkins clash! And when the doors are open to the living and dining rooms, the mismatched palettes strike a discordant note.

The point is, if you always gravitate to one or two colors, stick with them. Look in your closet. If most of your clothing is blue, it's a good indication that blue is your color—the one that always calls to you. You may admire red when your best friend wears it, but what looks great on her may not suit you when you put it on.

 *green*

GREEN is tranquil, nurturing, rejuvenating. It is a psychological primary, and because it is mixed from yellow and blue, it can appear both warm and cool. Time seems to pass more quickly in green rooms. Perhaps that's why waiting rooms off-stage are called "green rooms."

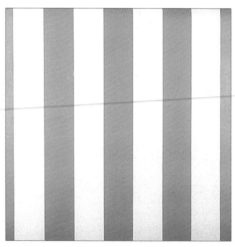

 *pink*

PINK is perceived as outgoing and active. It's also a color that flatters skin tones. Hot shades are invigorating, while soft, toned-down versions can be relaxed and charming.

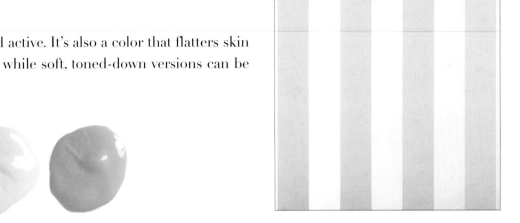

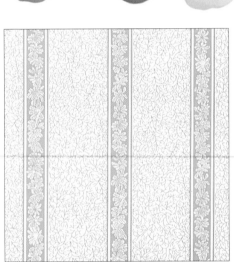

neutrals

GRAY goes with all colors—it is a good neighbor. Various tones of gray range from dark charcoal to pale oyster.

BLACK (technically the absence of color) enhances and brightens other colors, making for livelier decorating schemes when used as an accent.

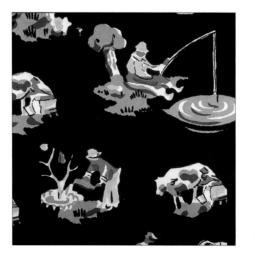

orange

ORANGE is energetic and sometimes overpowering when used full-force, but it has lovely softer sides as well. Like red, orange stimulates the appetite; that's why so many fast-food restaurants use it in their decor and logo. Because orange is so vibrant, it requires some contrasts to cool it down.

C O L O R S

The color wheel is a tool decorators use to see the relationship of one color to another. The primary colors (yellow, blue, and red) are combined in the remaining hues (orange, green, and purple). Neighboring colors harmonize and blend into one another, just as voices do in harmony. Complementary colors—those opposite one another on the color wheel—offer contrast and enhance one another. Colors that are not complementary make each other less true—blue and green become teal, for example.

CHAPTER 3

PATTERN & PRINT

One of the biggest dilemmas concerning decorating a room is how to use pattern and print: **how much** is too much? Like a conductor leading **a symphony** orchestra, you're striving for harmony, not cacophony. And yet a little dissonance can add some **much-needed zest**, like the right spice in a recipe. Too often we have a tendency to be too coordinated. When you try to make everything match, the result can look like alphabet soup. Sure the *L*s, *P*s and *Z*s are in there, but **mixed together** the shapes all look the same. After years of all white in the world of home décor, empty minimalist environments are finally passé. There is currently **a renaissance** of pattern and print. In this chapter, you'll learn how to choose them and use them to your **home's best advantage**.

The curtain's toile de Jouy design provides an interesting counterpoint to the geometric checks and stripes used on the chair and wall in this room. The unexpected combination of several patterns is effective without being overwhelming, thanks, here, to a unifying color palette.

PATTERN IN THE BACKGROUND

I am a pattern person. Probably it is by dint of both nurture and nature. As a descendant of nineteenth-century Manhattanites, my family heirlooms were acquired in the Victorian era: Oriental rugs, Wedgwood dishes, Tiffany lamps, painted leather screens, needle-point chairs, and Hudson River paintings. I have memories of the homes of my parents, grandparents, and great-grandparents, full of striped velvet sofas, silk damask drapes, Oriental carpets, toile wallcoverings, summer-porch slipcovers, and sisal mats in season. I remember changing slipcovers on the bamboo furniture with my grandmother, who showed me how to squeeze the backs of the cushions together and insert them just so into the faded floral summer covers. To forsake these memories and abandon this furniture would make me feel like a hypocrite. It is who I am. I have that very same bamboo furniture on my screened porch, covered in Motif Design's "Summer Porch" fabric.

All of these things have encouraged my love of patterns and prints. So has my own life experience. My first sofa was made of white canvas. First came love, then came marriage, then came me with the baby carriage, and . . . four children in all, not to mention a dog. The white canvas couch quickly became an embarrass-ment. Next, we bought our first home and stripped off all the offending wall-paper, thinking that a coat of white

A slightly faded summer stripe wears well on this vintage furniture.

paint would set the place right, only to discover that the walls were a disastrous labyrinth of cracks and crevices. Nothing short of a very expensive skim coat of plaster would conceal the mess. The walls still had lumps and bulges. The moldings and doors had so much paint buildup that they looked even worse by comparison. What could I do to hide my decrepit, albeit charming, walls? I hightailed it to the local wallpaper store where I was dismayed by the lack of selection. This was a long time ago—the 1970s. Wallcoverings had deteriorated in both popularity and design during the 1960s and 1970s. They had gone mod. Long out of fashion were the intricate historical patterns: the chinoiseries, toiles, Jacobeans, and tickings that had graced our ancestors' homes

This chair is covered in an elegant chinoi-serie (Chinese-inspired) pattern.

My immediate reaction was "I can do better than this!"

since the seventeenth century. My immediate reaction was "I can do better than this," and a career was born.

I began designing, and my husband and I began producing wallcoverings, one screen at a time. Being a decorator, a homeowner, and a mother, I vowed to design patterns that would fit into today's world . . . my world. Patterns that would coordinate with bathroom tiles both new and old, like mine. Prints that coordinated with the carpets and colors toward which we all gravitate,

The blue fleur-de-lis wallpaper ties in with the houndstooth sofa.

really livable designs based on classic references. Too often patterns seem to emerge from some design sanctum that has no connection with reality whatsoever. As a decorator and a consumer, I know how they wear and how they wear out in terms of use and appearance.

Our first wallcovering has a small fleur-de-lis design pirated from one of my family's old Oriental rugs. I hung it in my hall. Today I use a similar design there. I still love it. What's wrong with that? I wore jeans then and still wear them now. My goal was to create patterns that work and never date themselves. Quickly I discovered that if I was going to design wallcoverings I might as well design fabrics, too. A career expanded.

WHY YOU NEED PATTERN

We tend to think that an absence of pattern is restful. Quite the contrary. Our eyes need something on which to focus. A blank wall causes the eye to overwork in search of a focal point. In addition to giving our eyes a rest, pattern hides a multitude of sins. Got a dumpy couch or chair? Give it a "shabby chic" slipcover with an old-fashioned print. Got a straight-laced boxy chair? Soften its lines with a wonderful paisley print. Boxed pipes in a corner? Wrap your room in a wallpaper print, and the box will simply disappear. A windowless hall? Add a print, and it comes to life. Pattern can be the main event, or it can be the perfect accessory.

On and Off the Wall

Wallpaper is a concealer and a distraction. Wallpaper can even mask the shape of an awkward room. In addition to camouflaging bad lines and design details, patterned wallpaper also hides soil, stains, spots, scratches, scuff marks, and the general wear and tear of life. Nothing will make that dirty white canvas sofa look better than accessorizing it with a couple of printed throw pillows. And nothing will mask your dingy, drab bath tile better than

contrasting wallpaper. Clients Judy and John, just wallpapered their son's bath. We used a multicolored foulard (small print) wallpaper on a dark denim background. As Judy and John walked me through their recent round of redos, they exclaimed that this bath was the "real transformation." Not only do the tiles seem fresh and new, but the room looks bigger. How can that be? Darker walls look claustrophobic, right? *No.* The dramatic contrast created by the dark-color background on the wallpaper gives the formerly all-white bath presence and personality. It's no longer just a small bland bathroom off a boy's bedroom. Now it has its own identity.

In an older bath, I used pattern to hide flaws in walls.

A pretty country floral print camouflages the odd shape of this room.

A classic motif looks right at home in this breakfast room.

A miniprint lends a cozy touch surrounding this wall nook.

Customers are always surprised when pattern actually enlarges the space. They mistakenly assume pattern will make a room appear smaller. Hang wallpaper in the stair landing, and suddenly the space becomes a room, a reading nook, a spot to linger. Use wallpaper with a pattern on both walls of a tiny vestibule, and the ceiling and the hall beyond it will open up like a glorious valley after you've come through the mountain tunnel. You will understand that they are two separate spaces, with different purposes. If you treat them identically, the vestibule will disappear into the hall and become invisible.

Where to Use Strong Pattern

Obviously we can't use strong pattern everywhere. Overpowering pattern works best in measured doses. Use it only in small rooms or areas with short periods of usefulness—for example, the vestibule. After all, you only walk through it, no lingering here. A strong pattern will create a sense of space. Another appropriate place is a powder room. All too often this much-used room is at the center of the house. Mine is next to the front door. I am literally 15 feet from the doorbell. A strong pattern makes the space feel private and farther away from the central stair and front door. In these two areas, the only place you can decorate is on the wall. There's no furniture to romance the space, so say it with patterned wallpaper.

Dining Room. This dining room is another area that can take strong pattern. Let's be honest. How many hours a year is this room used? Perhaps 30? I'd call that a short period in the life of a year. Dining rooms are filled with wood: table, buffet, china cabinets, and chairs. It's a forest of wooden legs—sometimes more than 50. The rug is concealed under the forest of legs for the most part. Chair seats, if upholstered, are tucked under the table. Need to soften up the room? Add strong wallpaper. Mine is a Jacobean floral on a black background. The paper incorporates all the colors of my multiple sets of mismatched china and an assemblage of tablecloths. I can bring out the red, the green, or the gold depending on the time of year of my whim. Keep in mind that dining rooms are mostly fall and winter rooms. During those seasons we celebrate multiple holidays and rich colors predominate, whereas in summer, we picnic, barbecue, and eat outdoors.

Guest Room. Once again pattern engenders a sense of privacy. My guest room is a repository for cast-off furnishings. Now outfitted in matching paper and fabric, it has a certain élan, a kind of irreverent charm. The pattern unified all of the mismatched odd bits of furniture. I wouldn't want to live in this room 365 days a year, but my guests never fail to remark on its unique charm.

Laundry and Transition Rooms. These places often house a pile and a jumble of stuff, but they are also very utilitarian. Why not wallpaper them? It gives these rooms a little attitude and hopefully takes the drudgery out of the tasks performed within.

Like the vestibule, transition "rooms" aren't destinations, just means to a destination. For example, I have a small pantry that links the study, dining room, kitchen, mudroom, and basement stairwell. It's really a hall, not a true pantry. With much trepidation, I wallpapered it in a hot pink chinoiserie scenic print. Mostly it's just bits of wallpaper framing the multiple entrances that chop into every surface. Let's talk adorable. Let's talk love. To look at it all day—no way. But to breeze by and say hi—what fun. Now my hall deserves a name. It is the pantry. Another transition room might be between a bedroom and bath or a hall and a child's bedroom.

DECK THE WALLS

There are other areas of the home that warrant wallpaper, too. Back to our first real home, the one we owned as opposed to those we rented for a year or two, where a quick coat of paint had done the job. This time we stayed long enough to discover that "landlord white" doesn't last. My narrow stairwell, albeit lighted at the end by a beautiful stained glass window, looked like a scratched and scarred wreck after two years. We had outstayed our paint job. Suitcases had dinged the walls, my toddler's smeared fingerprints attested to her inability to reach

You can add personality to a plain room with wallpaper.

A strong pattern perks up this laundry room.

paper. Use a climbing Jacobean vine or an elegant wide salon stripe to emphasize the vertical height of a hall. Halls generally take a lot of paper, and you *can* use a strong pattern. Contrasting backgrounds are great, but in confined color combinations. You don't want a confetti look. And avoid overblown multicolored patterns. My hall touches virtually every room in the house. The hall pattern has to be a good neighbor to all of the other rooms with which it intersects. The multicolored Jacobean in my dining room, which adjoins only the hall and the pantry, would look awful next to my boys' bedrooms, or mine for that matter. Whereas the wallpaper in my hall, an off-white feather set within a creamy white lattice on a Sage background, is a wonderful neighbor. Quiet? Yes. Bland? No.

the railing, laundry baskets had scuffed the walls, pull toys had nicked the woodwork. Guess why they have wallpaper in hotel hallways? It is washable, and they wear well. Wallcoverings are simply more durable than paint. Wallpaper protects the walls from damage. Depending on the quality of the paper, you can scrub it quite thoroughly as long as you don't use abrasive cleanser that will scrub away the pattern. But most spray cleaners are fine.

Halls

Because halls are high-traffic areas and often narrow, they don't need much furniture. It would create only obstacles for people moving to and fro. But that doesn't mean that a hall should be undecorated. Instead, hang the wall with pictures, paintings, and wall-

A mudroom appears less utilitarian with a cheerful print.

A washable vinyl wallcovering is practical in a kitchen.

You can use a large-scale print in halls; in fact the large scale of the space welcomes a larger scale pattern. Tiny prints look wimpy and repeat too often. Halls also generally incorporate more architecture than any other room in the house: balustrades, railings, newel posts, and the sheer power and geometry of the stairs themselves. They need contrast, but keep the colors confined and don't overstate them. From light to dark is too strong. Halls need medium-value colors contrasted with light colors.

Kitchens

Kitchens also cry out for wallpaper. First, there is the maintenance factor: you can easily wash away spattered soap and grime from a vinyl wallcovering, whereas a painted surface sometimes shows a ring after spot-cleaning. Secondly, like the dining room and the hall, the kitchen is usually a room of few furnishings. No sofas, no chairs, no curtains. Plus, there are lots of hard surfaces on the floor, countertops, and cabinets. Add in the machinery, the stainless-steel appliances, and where's the warmth? You know where: the wallpaper. Kitchen wall space is usually limited, often confined to the soffit (the area above the upper cabinets) and small areas framing the doors. In the kitchen, a smaller, tighter pattern is preferable. Often there are only 12 to 20 inches above the cabinets. If your wallpaper choice has an 18-inch repeat (the size of the pattern before it's repeated), you will see only one element at most. If a pattern is too spread out, the repeat is interrupted and thus the rhythm is uneven, which hampers the cozy, unifying effect wallpaper is meant to have.

A kitchen wallcovering can be anything from a two-color geometric to a multicolored fruit print. I personally prefer a multicolored pattern as I think it rounds up all the disparate colors that inevitably multiply in the kitchen among the dishes, napkins, message centers, backpacks, towels, and food packaging. When sampling kitchen wallpaper, climb onto a counter, and station your sample where it will be viewed, which usually means above the upper cabinets. Make sure your choice reads well from a distance.

Bathrooms

I've owned three homes and 18 bathrooms, and except for my current powder room, I have never changed a tile or a vanity unless I have been forced to because of a leak. Inevitably, I look at my sometimes pristine, sometimes dreary vintage baths and think about gutting and remodeling them. Ultimately, I do the math and decide that if they still function well, I will make them work. For me that always means wallpaper. In my son's bath, an old mosaic

"The hall pattern has to be a good neighbor to all of the other rooms with which it intersects."

floor looks fresh and up-to-date with a small red-and-black tartan-plaid paper and black-and-white gingham curtains. In my daughter's bath, a clawfoot tub and black-slate countertop looks clean and crisp with a vintage black-and-white paper and crisp white linen curtains on a black rod. In our bath, a soft green fern on a creamy ground makes my faded white tile look cheery.

It was only in the powder room, when confronted with swirly yellow plastic laminate countertops and a shell-shaped sink that I tore it all out and installed replacements, a wood floor and a black background print. Of all our wallpapers, my son tells me this is his favorite.

You Get It by Now. Use wallpaper where you can't furnish: hall, bath, and kitchen. Hang it in places where you need pattern and print to soften hard furnishings and features such as cabinets or stairs. Use wallpaper where maintenance and wear are an issue or where walls are bumpy. If your walls are really bad, use a textured paper or a weave, a chevron, or a small, tight pattern. Then the paper becomes a surface to mask the damage.

Always get a large sample to bring home; then situate it at different places from where it will be viewed. I had two samples of my hall wallpaper. One I put alternately near the entrances to the living and dining rooms, the other at the top of the stairs for the distant view. That way I

Try out various samples by taping them onto the wall.

could see how the color and pattern would look from up close and from far away.

MASTERING THE MIX WITH FABRIC

In the furniture chapter, beginning on page 122, I talk about how to determine quality seating and how to judge whether your sofa or chair will last. And I address proportion, both how the furniture will fit in your room and how your physical frame will fit in the furniture. These are all relevant criteria. Yet no single component is more important in defining the perception of your seating and you

than the fabric you select. Your furniture is judged by those who neither sit in it very frequently nor scrutinize it to see how it holds up over time. It is most often the patterns and prints of the fabrics upon which friends and extended family remark. Fabrics are so much a part of our daily lives that they become our environment.

Pattern can add character to a boring couch or a lumpy old chair. A floral print can convert a featureless bedroom into a comforting retreat. But do we dare? Do we use a single toile pattern to set the whole mood, or should we play it safe and go with solids and use pattern as an accent only? And after we've selected a pattern, do we take the next bold step and mix more than one? And don't certain patterns work well together? Just as with apparel, certain combinations are natural partners: a paisley mixed with a rich tartan plaid, a homespun ticking paired with a calico

Fabric with a subtle print emphasizes the shape of furniture.

floral or a toile and a gingham check. I've already discussed pattern in terms of walls, but what about pattern and the furnishings? Let's talk about fabric.

WHERE NOT TO USE WALLPAPER

The living room and master bedroom are sometimes propositions. Don't wallpaper the family room, because there's already too much going on in terms of flooring, sofas, pillows, bookcases, built-ins, and electronics. Don't wallpaper the computer room, which needs to be a rather quiet space. If the walls of either of these rooms are in dreadful condition, then choose a muted print.

Making a Selection

There are so many wonderful options from which to choose: damask, corduroy, linen, floral, paisley, stripe, check, foulard, silk, viscose, rayon, brocade, toile, tapestry. Fabric selection can seem bewildering. How are we to know not only how a fabric will look but how it will wear? How will that tiny swatch look when all 28 yards have been upholstered on my sofa? How will that small sample look when 42 yards are made into curtains hanging on three

Bring home a fabric swatch if you're trying to coordinate patterns.

walls of my living room? Overwhelming or picture-perfect?

The Ready-Made Option. With the emergence of today's lifestyle stores and dot-com options, it's easy to buy ready-made sofas, chairs, and even window treatments. The fabric has been preselected and purchased in bulk by the manufacturer. The sofa, chair, or curtain is sold "as is." Thus, some of the guesswork is eliminated. You can see an actual sofa covered in the print. Still you must take home a swatch or, even better, an actual pillow from the piece of furniture or a panel of the curtains to see how it reads in your house. (Usually if you leave an imprint of your credit card, the store will let you take the pillow at closing and return it upon opening the next day.) That way everyone in the family can put in their two cents. Just as paint doesn't look the same on your wall as it did on the paint chip in the store, so pattern changes from store to home. Camel cotton duck that you thought would be so right against your sisal carpet looks orange when combined with Seagrass. Or the paisley print that was for your study swarms like a plate full of spaghetti when next to the Oriental rug. Patterns have a mind of their own.

The Swatch Test. Nothing is certain except death and taxes, but you sure can reduce your risk of making a wrong choice by looking at the swatch in your home. Don't lay it on the floor, unless that's how you intend to use it. Rather, drape it over a chair. For a curtain, hang the sample at the window, making sure to gather the fabric if it is to be gathered or pleat it if it will be pleated. A pattern with a distinct repeat, even one as uncomplicated as a bold stripe, can become distorted or lopsided when it doesn't lay or hang flat or if it is gathered. It's smart to use painter's tape to hang your sample on a wall or the window trim; that way you won't take the paint off with it when you remove the sample.

Practicalities of Pattern

When selecting a fabric to cover a piece of seating, ask yourself whether you want to flaunt the furniture or camouflage its imperfections. A solid color will leave the clear and evident shape of your furniture uncompromised by print or pattern. Like a freshly pressed white shirt, it had better be immaculate. It has to have good bones and correct proportions. If your furniture is a bit on the marginal side, use pattern and print to trick the eye into thinking the furniture is better than it actually is. On the other hand, if you are asking your furniture to do something it was not really intended for (for example, turning a former living room chair into a guest room chair), go the print-and-pattern route. Use a print to masquerade the

"A pattern with a distinct repeat, even one as uncomplicated as a bold stripe, can become distorted or lopsided when rouched."

"If your furniture is a bit on the marginal side, use pattern and print to trick the eye into thinking the furniture is better than it actually is."

club chair proportions, and make the piece look more like a lady's boudoir chair. Pattern allows us to cast furniture against type. A large floral fabric will do wonders to mask the boxy shape of your husband's frat-room couch, and a ticking stripe will lend a cozy country feeling to an early apartment-life sectional sofa.

Use versus abuse. Pattern is made for situations that will get a lot of use. With four children and an excessively drooly dog, I cannot subject myself to the stress of high-maintenance fabrics. I recently re-covered my one kitchen armchair. It's a wonderful curbside find and a much-coveted seat for watching morning cartoons. The old fabric, a dark plaid, was more than 25 years old. It finally wore through. I replaced the plaid with a small-print, medium-color woven material. After only two years, the fabric is dirty. That old plaid camouflaged a lot of use, that the new solid fabric did not. My new dining room chairs came covered in white muslin. In the interests

of short-term economy, I left them that way. But even with infrequent use, the fabric lasted a mere three years. Now they are covered in a woven wool paisley. It will last for generations. Again and again, we learn that a short-sighted economy only costs more in the long run. My tablecloth is made from the same wool paisley. I leave it on from November to March. A wipe with a damp sponge

Used generously, toile looks dramatic and formal.

keeps it clean and fresh. How many times could I reuse a white tablecloth without laundering and pressing it? Pattern makes for easy care.

More lessons I learned. I do have one piece of furniture in my home covered in a solid: a beautiful English sofa in my bedroom. It's adorned with Bridgewater arms, handsome turned legs, and a tight back and seat. It's perfection, and the solid-taupe velvet fabric that covers it shows its beautiful bones to advantage. The only time I sit on the sofa is after a bath. Too lazy to towel-dry, I prefer to drip-dry in my tired terrycloth robe with a stack of magazines at hand. It is one of my indulgences during a few idle moments. Guess what? The velvet scars. That's a fabric vocabulary word you should know; it is one I should have remembered. Scarring means that the imprint of your body remains on the surface of the fabric when you sit on it. I also have a shield-back chair from my grandmother—it's of good quality but nothing very stylish.

Plaid strikes a casual note in the family room.

I've upholstered it in a striped floral print. I sit on it and stand on it (wearing shoes) to get at my upper cabinets. Ten years later, it looks good as new, whereas my English sofa is to be admired but not used. Perfection I achieved; usage I did not address.

Be practical. Our relationship with our furniture is a long-term commitment. When deciding whether to cover a piece of furniture in a print or a solid fabric, address the use of the piece and its beauty. How much time and money do you want to invest in maintaining the fabric? My friend swears by white. This is the right choice for her, but it's completely wrong for me. Except for

Three different prints—all in brown and white—work well together.

the living room. I could dynamite this room, and no one would notice because we use it so infrequently. But the family room sectional should be made practically of woven steel. As a young decorator, I met with a client who had three young sons. When I inquired as to what she would like to cover the family room sofa, she requested woven steel. I now know why.

MIXED MESSAGES

The old rule of thumb was that you had to choose between pattern on the walls, the furniture, or the floor. A patterned carpet meant using a solid or a near solid couch. To a large extent that still holds true, although the rules are less ironclad today. The lines are blurring. My computer room has a kilim rug, foulard curtains, a striped foulard wallpaper above the dark wood paneling, two tightly woven striped upright chairs, and a damask club chair and ottoman. A lot of pattern, yes. Busy, no. All of the colors are deep and of equal value; thus the overall effect is quiet and subdued. The damask and the tight stripe almost read as solids. The foulard and the foulard stripes are evenly repeating geometric companions. All of these prints complement the ethnic kilim rug, and all are natural companions to one another.

How To Make It Work

In my dining room, the wallpaper I chose is a climbing Jacobean-inspired floral pattern printed on a black background. An intricate Oriental rug (a family heirloom) is on

An intricate Oriental carpet can be successfully paired with other patterns.

finally asked then-seven-year-old Erik for his opinion. He replied, "Clearly number three." I had found my fabric ally. Number nine was a perfectly fine choice, but number three was better. If you have no gift for pattern or print, find out who within your circle does. But I believe the ability to see the right choice is there within each of us, for the most part. When you're looking at a print, let yourself respond. Don't think, feel. And find your ally. My children said I just picked the youngest child who could speak and made him agree with me. If you can't convince anyone in the household, try reasoning with the dog.

I taped numerous plaid samples over my window before choosing this one.

the floor. Too much next to each other, I separated them with a solid-color painted dado. Now the look is balanced and just right. No mix-and-match rules are actually broken. In my family room, a quiet glenplaid sectional in Olive, Mustard, and Pimiento sits on a tweedy Olive rug chosen to hide burns from fire embers and stains from everyday living.

Trust yourself. When choosing a pattern, follow your instincts and find your ally. In my house, it is my son Erik. Once, when trying to choose a plaid valance for the kitchen, I had 11 samples taped over the window. Everyone from my mother to my housekeeper liked number nine, whereas I liked number three. Desperate, I

Narrowing Down Your Choices

Start by selecting fabric for the principal piece of furniture in a room. In the bedroom, it's the bed; in the family room, it's the sofa, for example. Choose a major pattern colorway, and keep it dominant. Too much of a secondary color theme, and the room gets spotty looking. Gradually layer in other fabrics on the supporting furniture players. Be playful only with the minor accents: throw pillows, footstools, accessories. Playful gets unfunny fast.

Combining patterns is more about scale and proportion than quantity, so just as with solid colors, it is easier to contrast than to match. You might be inclined to think that a berber or sisal carpet would look best with a small-patterned fabric. But when you put them together, the very weave of the carpet itself and the small fabric pattern start to "beehive." They swarm and multiply. All of a sudden, subtle becomes busy and quiet becomes loud. Whereas a large-scale plaid sits solidly on a small-weave carpet. Marrying like patterns is complicated. As a rule of thumb: big on the floor means small on the sofa. Small on the floor means big on the sofa.

Window treatments. I have preached the virtues of pattern repeatedly—except on the windows. Labor is expensive, and yardage quantities are excessive. Your carpet will wear out, and your uphol-stery will change—all the while the same window treatments will remain. I

Balance large patterns with small ones.

like a solid or a texture at the windows. An exception might be a floral print in a bedroom.

WHAT TO USE WHERE

So, now you know what looks right, but what wears right? When I polled people about their fabric conundrums and consternations, they weren't as concerned with selecting the pattern as with judging the quality. My friend JoAnn said that her sofa had not worn well. It was an expensive piece by a well-known designer and upholstered in his porch floral fabric. JoAnn felt she should have gotten

I recommend a solid fabric for most window treatments.

more out of the fabric than it delivered. But the fabric is tea-colored linen floral, and linen does not have good abrasion ratings. Quite simply, that means it wears out faster than cotton, for example.

To help you determine how to select an appropriate pattern in terms of both appearance and quality, I've compiled a list of fabric patterns and terms along with guidelines for using them appropriately.

Abrasion Resistance. This is the fabric's ability to resist wear from rubbing. It contributes to durability.

Fibers that absorb water are easier to clean. Stains on slick nonabsorbent fibers are more stubborn. All natural fibers from animals and vegetables are hydrophilic, as are

SYNTHETIC
IS NO LONGER A DIRTY WORD

Fibers can be natural (cotton, linen, silk, wool) or synthetic (rayon, polyester). Fibers all have different properties. When choosing a fiber, judge the way the fabric feels when you handle it. Don't get hung up on natural versus synthetic. Often fabrics are a blend of 35 percent cotton, 15 percent linen, and 50 percent polyester, for example. Usually the cotton and linen are on the front of the fabric, the part you interact with, whereas the synthetic is on the back, providing support and strength. My motto is that if you have to ask what the fiber is when you feel it, it is natural feeling enough.

two synthetic fibers: rayon and acetate. That means they absorb water and thus clean more easily. Polyester and nylon are not in this group. Remember the polyester shirts from the 1970s with the permanently yellowed half circles under the arms? These fabrics don't breathe, and they make you feel too warm. Besides cleanability, hydrophilics are more comfortable next to your skin.

Brocade. A weighty fabric woven of silk, cotton, wool, or a combination. A raised, floral design (called a *jacquard*) is its distinguishing feature. Brocade is often used for upholstery and draperies.

Chenille. Typically a cotton, chenille is looped with a protruding pile. It can be used for upholstery and pillows.

Chintz. Chintz is a glazed cotton. Chintzing is a form of finishing; it gives the fabric a slight sheen. Over time and washing, the chintz wears off. I would not recommend chintz for an area that gets heavy use, but it's great for window treatments, the occasional chair, or a seldom-used sofa.

Cotton. A natural fiber with good abrasion resistance, good draping ability, and a soft hand.

Damask. This is a pattern made of heavy reversible fine yarns of cotton, silk, or wool. Damask has been woven for over five centuries. It is a classic look that works well on

Patterned, washable cottons are perfect for bed linens and curtains.

on seating pieces. Although lattice-like in design, a five-star repeat comes up more as a centerpiece when it is upholstered on a chair or sofa.

Lace. Typically, it is cotton or cotton-polyester blend material featuring open-work designs. Lace is frequently used for curtains.

Linen. This fabric has strength but poor abrasion resistance. Linen is not as durable as cotton, nor does it drape well. However, linen feels nice to the touch, but because it wrinkles easily, it isn't a smart choice for covering seating pieces.

Matelasse. This is a medium- to heavy-weight, luxurious double cloth with a blistered or quilted surface.

upholstered seating pieces as well as on draperies.

Duck. Duck is a closely woven cotton or linen. It is durable and slightly lighter in weight than canvas. Use it for upholstery or slipcovers.

Five-Star Repeat. Many of today's fabrics are designed around the standard ready-made sofa or chair-pillow size and have what is called a five-star layout. When cut and sewn, the five stars or points of the design each center on a pillow. These five-star patterns are very effective used

Muslin. A course, plain-weave cotton in white or cream. It is often sheer and not as heavy as duck. Use it for sheeting, curtains, and light slipcovers.

Overall. This is a term for a pattern that is even and overall or random. Although this type of design gives good camouflage to stains and spills, I think its lack of direction makes it a less-attractive choice for seating pieces. An overall pattern works best for curtains.

Self Patterns. This term is used to describe a fabric wherein the weave creates a pattern. An example of a self-pattern fabric is damask, which is widely used for draperies. Another is brocade, which is used for upholstery.

Silk. Silk is traditionally a natural fiber, but today it often contains strong, durable synthetic fibers as well. Taffeta silk is smooth and has a sheen. Shantung silk is dull, slightly rough, and looks more like linen.

Silk has excellent drape and a luxurious hand. It is the thinnest of natural fibers and can be washed. However, silk does not have good abrasion resistance, and its springback is poor. Although it fades in direct sunlight, silk makes wonderful curtains and draperies, but only if they are stationary.

These tonal-patterned cotton cushions resemble silk.

Stripes should line up perfectly on front and back cushions.

for dining chairs with wood frames. The frame allows the stripe to be presented at its best: straight and unadulterated. Stripes don't take kindly to bends or curves. A stripe on a chair seat and back must run perpendicular to the chair arms, creating a secondary pattern that will not match up.

Don't cover a sectional sofa in a stripe as I once did. What a shock! The stripe ran parallel to only one flank of the sectional and was perpendicular to the other. I kept rotating the corner cushion trying to see what looked better. Answer: nothing. On the other hand, stripes do work well on walls, beds, armless chairs, wood-frame chairs, and couches.

Tapestry. This is a heavy, ribbed, colored jacquard design made of wool and silk that is used for upholstery.

Stripes. Stripes are versatile and timeless. They can be formal or informal. Use stripes with caution, as all the sides, seat, or back cushions cannot always line up, especially on an entire sofa. This may create a jarring mismatch in places. On the other hand, stripes are an ideal choice

Ticking. Ticking is strong, closely woven cotton that usually has stripes. Guess where the name came from? The woven fabric was meant to keep the feathers in the pillows and let the bloodsucking ticks out. Use it for curtains or slipcovers.

Toile de Jouy. An eighteenth-century cotton or linen fabric printed with pastoral scenes. It was first produced in the French town of Jouy, hence its name. Use toile for curtains and upholstery. (See the swatch, below.)

A lively paisley motif can trace its design roots to ancient India.

This quilted coverlet is made of 100-percent cotton.

Wool. This natural fiber can be scratchy and expensive. Wool is not for the family room couch, but it is fine for the less-used study chair.

Woven Fabrics. These fabrics are made by weaving two sets of yarns at right angles to each other to create complex designs. Two examples are damask and brocade. Woven fabrics wear better than plain weaves. That's why they're good for upholstery and curtains.

New dyes and technology offer endless possibilities for decorating with pattern and print.

CHAPTER 4

WINDOW TREATMENTS

W ith 20 years of decorating experience, I am still **sometimes intimidated by** window treatments. Even the term "window treatments" is off-putting. It sounds "clinical," like applying therapy to an ailment. "Window dressing" is no better — it seems frivolous. The truth is, window treatments are perhaps **the most problematic and confusing** component in the decorating package. Because the process of **choosing the right window treatments** can be **intricate**, people prefer to think they can do without them. Many clients have told me, "Oh, I don't need window treatments, I have **beautiful light**." But what appears to be a **gorgeous sun-dappled room** during the day can look like a box with a big black hole at night. When other people say, "I don't need window treatments because I have no neighbors," I tell them about a client of mine named Nancy.

Windows are an important architectural element in terms of style and function. With the right treatment, they can act as a beautiful focal point in a room.

"Window treatments don't have to be excessive . . . but they can be decorative and lush if you like."

Nancy's new multi-jet whirlpool tub sits inside a beautiful bay window that overlooks her six acres on the water in Greenwich, Connecticut. The nearest neighbor seems a million miles away. One fine weekday morning with the kids at school, Nancy decided to take a luxurious soak, relaxing with aromatherapy, wafting music, and liberal doses of bath salts. After half an hour, Nancy stood up—and locked eyes with the garbage collector. She said she didn't know who was more embarrassed: he or she. Nancy now has beautiful lace half-curtains that protect her privacy and allow natural light to filter inside the room. So you see, it doesn't take a stalker or a Peeping Tom with a telescope to realize that most of us need some form of window treatments.

A simple café curtain addresses privacy while revealing the handsome details of this bathroom's windows.

Choosing a design would be a lot less stressful if you didn't think of window treatments as a big deal, although in many ways they are. Window treatments can be eye-catching. As the largest vertical element in a room, they naturally draw attention. But window treatments don't have to be excessive—all that light and air eclipsed by yards of fabric—but they can be decorative and lush if you like. Formal designs (what I call "3-D treatments") are often three layers deep and include a decorative valance or swag and stationary panels that hang on the outermost part of the window; a daytime privacy component consisting of a sheer, half-curtain or a shutter; and an inner layer offering total privacy at night in the form of a black-out roller shade or an opaque cellular or pleated shade. That's a lot of layers, money, options, and decisions.

If your taste is for something less complicated, window treatments can be simple and streamlined. In this chapter, you'll learn the language of window treatments and how to make specific recommendations for what to use where, according to your taste, needs, and budget. There are no hard-and-fast rules, but I can offer some useful guidelines.

GENERAL CONSIDERATIONS

With window treatments, function is just as important as form, if not more so. You need something that is attractive and easy to use and wears well. Start by addressing the practical issues: Will the material provide the desired degree of privacy as well as light? Will the fabrics hold up to the sun? Is the pattern and repeat appropriate to the size of the windows? Is the material the right weight? Is it

"Does the look complement the style of your house?
The rest of your furnishings?
The architecture and shape of your windows?"

light enough to drape or hang gracefully, or is it heavy and bulky? Is the cost within your budget? (Window treatments require a lot of fabric.) Is it easily adjustable?

Aesthetics. Next move on to what is appropriate for the room and your home. Does the look complement the style of your house? The rest of your furnishings? The architecture and shape of your windows? Be sure to consider the time of day you use the room most — daytime or evening — and the room's exposure. For example, south- or west-facing rooms get lots of sunlight, which may need to be controlled if you use the rooms during the day, particularly in the afternoon. But north- or east-facing rooms used during the day cannot afford to lose one iota of light. At night the exposure is irrelevant, but the amount of black, empty glass is.

Insulation. What condition are your windows in? Can they benefit from the insulation window treatments can provide? Appropriately lined curtains or shades can help keep a room warm or cool. But some window treatments (such as heavy lined panels) can cut off the airflow from a radiator or an air conditioner. If there are windy spots, blinds and louvers ("hard treatments") will clang and

clatter whenever the window is open. Look for a soft alternative, such as a fabric shade.

Mechanics. Don't overlook the mechanics of the window treatment you've chosen. Will it work without banging a wall or scraping the window trim? If blinds are door-mounted, you don't want to grab them every time you reach for the doorknob. You may need hold-down brackets for blinds or tiebacks for your curtains. Certain kinds of shades for skylights and other inaccessible windows can be motorized and operated at the push of a button by remote control.

Before making any decisions, examine these issues. Then you'll be ready to choose from the many types and styles that are on the market.

From the Outside Looking In

Think about how your window treatments will look from the outside of your house, and aim for consistency. When I was a child, my mother always insisted that our home look good from the street, both for ourselves and for our neighbors. She often

Formal panels and a pleated valance suit a traditional room.

Cover the lower half of any window at street level.

railed against other people's window treatments. When I moved from my last house, I heard that my neighbor was pleased to see our large and active family go (four kids, photo shoots, grandparents living in a small house at the back). Well! For 11 years I had to put up with her window treatments: red blinds, blue blinds, sometimes nothing at all. From the street, they were hideous to see during the day and at night, while she got to look at

my wonderful white uniform shutters on the entire front face of my house. Mom was right.

Privacy Issues

For privacy it's important to screen at least the lower portion of a window above street level. But if your window is below street level, it will need covering from the top all the way down. If your windows are at eye level, lower privacy is more of a consideration. As my kids say about our neighbors who leave their shades up, "We can see their whole lives." That's why it's important to examine your window treatments from outside your home, at night as well as during the daylight hours. Additionally, it seems to me that when you are up and walking around and active, privacy is not as imperative as it is when you're sitting or reclining and more vulnerable.

Half-curtains. My strong bias is for half-curtains whenever daytime privacy is an issue. Even when you are walking around, only your head and shoulders will be exposed. I use half-shutters, and they suffice even in the bathroom. You can layer this look with something that descends, such as a Roman blind or a balloon or roller shade. If you have a top-down window treatment, the only way to create real privacy is with it completely lowered. Besides, at least a portion of what you see outside consists of sky or treetops. When a window treatment comes from the top down, it blocks off this

Partial covering may be adequate for an upstairs room.

prettiest of views. If you leave the treatment partially up, chances are all you may see are parked cars, driveways, and the street.

I treat the front of my house more rigorously than the back—shutters on front windows, little or nothing on the back ones. I don't need privacy in the kitchen because it backs onto my yard, and I don't sleep or bathe

A plaid pattern is a good choice for gathered curtains.

there. But I did add valances because I have a lot of glass, which can look very cold at night when it's left bare.

CURTAINS AND VALANCES

When it comes to choosing a curtain, it's your call. All kinds of fabric hang and drape differently. A sheer or lightweight fabric can be twisted and draped in one single piece over a pole, whereas a heavyweight fabric is only suitable for panels and valances. Some fabrics (such as

inexpensive cottons and linens) must be lined, or they'll look like bed sheets hanging from the window. Other fabrics (such as silks and taffetas) puddle beautifully. Still, you have to let your taste guide you. Remember when we were told to avoid heavy fabrics for window treatments? Guess what? Velvet panels have become the hottest item in the most trend-setting catalogs.

Pattern. What should you think about when you're selecting curtain fabric? First, choose the right-size pattern repeat. Curtains are usually gathered or pleated. The repeat of a large wide stripe can look lopsided and asymmetrical when gathered. A large empty repeat or a pattern with a large illustrative image can get lost and will break up — only part of the image will be visible. Use small patterns, stripes that are close together, or self patterns (such as damasks), homespun checks, or solids.

Another thing to keep in mind is that fabrics tend to fade in sunlight and with washing. If you hang curtains made of cheap material, they will look like your old laundry eventually. But the sun can destroy expensive fabric, too, especially if the material is fragile (such as an unlined silk) or if the dyes are not colorfast. Industry tests have shown that 90 percent of all window-treatment fading takes place in the first six weeks of exposure. If you can be patient, get a sample of the fabric, leave it on the windowsill, and see what happens.

Lining. If fading takes place, remember that a lining and an interlining can offer assistance. In addition to improving the way the curtain hangs, a *lining* helps to preserve the true color of the curtain's face fabric. Use a lining fabric that has been treated to resist rot and the damage caused by the sun and pollution. An *interlining* is a soft, blanket-like material that is sandwiched between the lining and the curtain fabric. Like a lining, it increases light-blocking qualities of the face fabric and extends the life of the curtain. The only downside to lining a curtain is the cost. But as my dad always says (and so do I, often), "You should only be unhappy once, when you pay the bill, not every time you use the product."

Sheers

As their name suggests, sheers are typically made of a translucent fabric, such as muslin, linen, gauze, or lace that offers daytime privacy but also lets in plenty of light. I think they are suitable for any window. Sheer fabric is generally inexpensive, and as the curtains are intended to be unlined, they don't incur the extra costs of lining, interlining, or additional labor. That's one reason why sheers are a good first layer. The rest of the layers can come whenever you are ready. Floor-length sheers usually look a little limp. But they do work well as a Roman shade, graceful and understated. Linen, muslin, and lace all appear whiter than the actual fabric sample when held up to the window. So don't worry if they are a bit more yellow than your window trim: against the light they will brighten up quite a bit. I think sheers should have some texture. If they are solid or opaque, they look like bed sheets. A nice texture diffuses the light and creates a soft silhouette.

While sheers obscure the view from the outside into your home during the day, at night they have the opposite effect. As the interior becomes brighter than the exterior, you can't see outside, but outsiders can see soft, unidentifiable shapes inside your home. The amount of ruching, or gathered fabric, determines the degree of privacy.

When using sheers, you often need more fabric than you think to get any degree of privacy. Sheer curtains shouldn't gather, billow, and fold. It is also a good idea to use weighted tape at the hem, too. This makes the curtain hang in place nicely.

Lace. Lace curtains are a favorite of mine for letting in light while obscuring a less-than-desirable view. Currently we are making lace panels to obscure an air shaft in a city co-op apartment. The sill-length panels will also conceal the window-mounted air conditioners for the 330 days a

Window Treatment Tips

▶ In general, I believe window treatments should be neutral. Curtains, especially those that are stationary, almost never become worn out. Other elements in the room will change, but your curtains will be just as you bought them, only dustier—so choose something for the long haul.

▶ Window treatments can take a lot of yardage, so their cost can be very price-sensitive vis-à-vis the cost per yard of the fabric. However, remember the labor cost is fixed regardless of the price of the fabric.

▶ A lining and an interlining improves the way a curtain hangs. You can sew individual weights or

a long, thin chain weight into the bottom hem to help the curtain hang evenly, too.

▶ In the dining room, the drama should center on the table and the meal. The windows are just supporting players, as they are in the bedroom. But in the living room, window treatments can take the spotlight. In a kitchen or bathroom, window treatments should be practical— not too many folds or pleats that will trap grime and odors.

▶ Window treatments can be easily overdone and overdressed. Let the fabric and the window speak for themselves.

A charming pairing of plaid and lace adds interest to a plain window.

year the units are not in use. When the air conditioners are in operation, the lace panels can be pulled to the side with a simple decorative hook.

Lace works best on small windows. The curtains needn't match or even be new. You can hang mismatched panels for an Old World look, and no one will notice. If they do, they'll think the look is charming. Remember, lace will be lighter and brighter at the window, so it's okay if the curtains are a bit yellowed with age.

Use drapery clips for a no-sew option, or sew a simple rod pocket at the top. A tension rod works fine for these light-

weight treatments. Usually the side edges of the fabric are prefinished with decorative scallops, so very little sewing is required.

Valances

I have a strong bias toward leaving windows clear and open and letting the light flood in, but that doesn't mean I don't like window treatments. I have them in almost every window in my home. For example, in my kitchen a ruched fabric creates a valance that skims the tops of the windows. A valance can come in a variety of styles: gathered in soft folds, flat, tailed, or in a more-formal version with one of a number of types of pleats.

Cornices. A cornice is a type of hard valance, made from wood or other sturdy material, that can be painted or covered in fabric or wallpaper. A cornice is usually wall-mounted above the window to hide the rods and the top of the curtain and window. Elaborately carved wooden cornices were the darlings of the eighteenth century, and

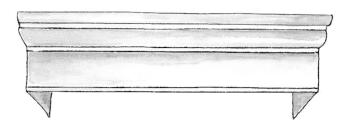

Cornice

Lambrequin

A simple tapered valance pulls this room together.

there are still many times when curtains look better finished when connected by a valance or cornice.

Lambrequin. A lambrequin is another type of hard valance that is made of stiffened fabric. A lambrequin extends not just over but down the sides of the window, sometimes even to the floor.

The Fancy Stuff: Swags and Jabots

Swags and jabots (also called cascades or tails) may look like one continuous element, but they should actually be

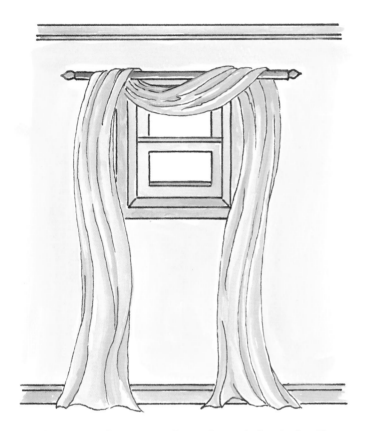

This swagged curtain makes a short window look tall.

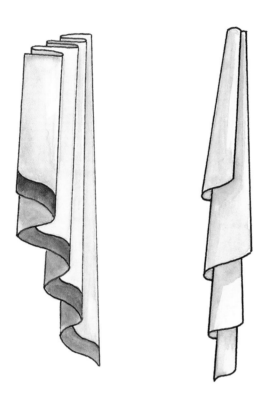

Jabots may have accordian pleats (left) or spiral pleats (right).

Trimmings and tassels will add pretty details and enhance the shape of a curtain.

made as separate pieces. *Swags* work best over individual windows, rather than miles of French doors or windows. It is very difficult to arrange a long wall of swags artfully, to say nothing of the overkill effect of doing so. Swags work as a sort of crown to a window. What is nice about them is that, like valances, you can mount them well above the window and make a low or short window look taller. (See the illustration, above.) Swags look great with trim, braid, or whatever will show off their pretty shape. Contrasting liners also work wonderfully on swags. Swags should extend beyond the width of

the windows so that they don't prevent sunlight from entering the room.

Jabots descend down the sides of a window from a swag. They come in many different sizes and shapes and can be single or double tailed, as they would in the case of a bay window or two abutting windows. Jabots can be accordion- or spiral-pleated. (See the illustrations, above.) They can be installed over or under the swag, although jabots should always be under swags to keep them from looking too stiff. Jabots must go at least halfway down the length of the curtain, if there is an undercurtain, or to the sill.

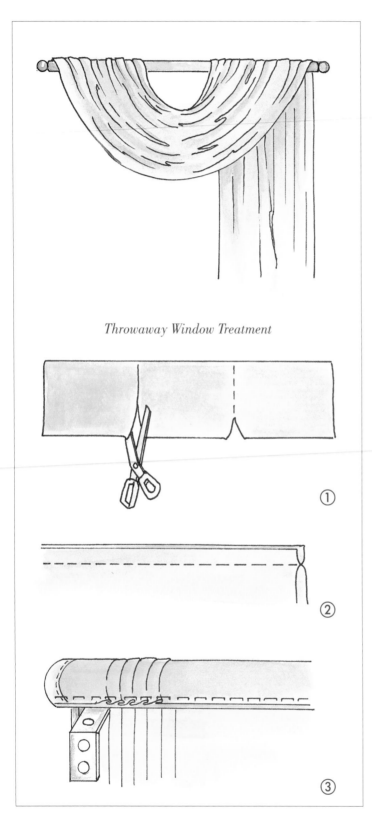

Throwaway Window Treatment

① ② ③

Because the lining on a swag-and-jabot treatment is visible, it should be carefully constructed. Use the face fabric or a contrasting lining, which looks dressier than plain old white cotton.

There are also swags that appear to be one single continuous piece of fabric simply wrapped around and draped across a pole — what I call throwaway window treatments. This works best with a lightweight or sheer fabric, such as muslin or linen, with no repeat or design. The lightness of the fabric means you really can twist and shape it. Although the drape of the fabric should hold it to the pole, sometimes a bit of double-stick tape or a piece of hook-and-loop-tape will help hold the fabric in place. The draped pole, while it seems very simple, has actually fooled many a home sewer. If you try to drape a single piece of fabric up and over and down, you will never get it to pleat nicely and lay correctly. Instead, ① cut the fabric into three sections — one for the top and two for the sides — which is easier to work with, ② and then sew the pieces together. ③ Seams can be hidden on the back of the pole. (See the illustration, left.)

Headings. The heading refers to how the curtain is attached to the pole or rod. There are many types of headings, including the typical, simple pinch-pleated type. (Refer to the illustrations, right.) A *rod pocket* is the simplest heading or attachment for curtains. Rod pockets cover the rod like a sleeve covers an arm, hiding all but the

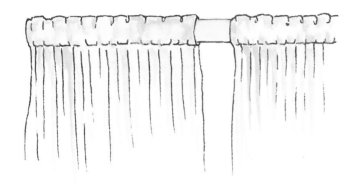

Rod-Pocket Heading

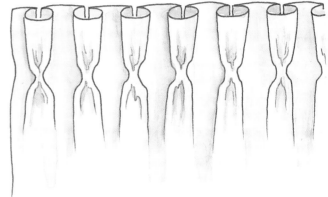

Goblet-Pleated Heading

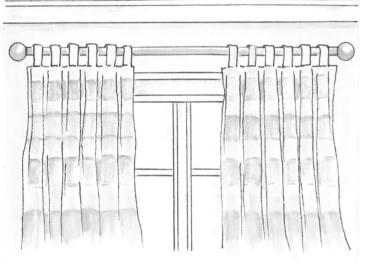

Tabbed Heading

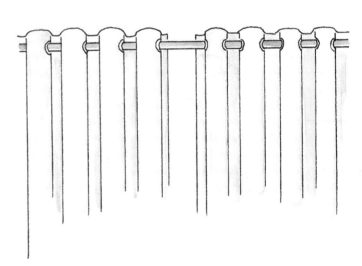

Pierced Heading

finial. And like a sleeve they can be gathered back, or ruched in window-dressing language. This heading works better for lightweight fabrics, as it is hard to push back a heavier fabric (just as you can keep your soft sweater sleeve pushed up, but your coat sleeve is another matter).

Goblet headings are pleats sewn into narrow tubes every few inches. They create supple folds of fabric down the length of the curtain. If you want fancy, this is an elegant look—very calculated and engineered.

Tabs are another option. The Shaker-style heading shown above left uses tabs or ties made from the same fabric to attach the curtains to the rod. Still another type, a *pierced heading* can be created with grommets for a clean, contemporary look when paired with a metal rod.

Finishing Details

Borders or trim on window treatments emphasize shape or form. Borders can be made from almost anything—flat tape, trim, braid, cord, ribbon, fringe, gimp or piping sewn on in an outline, or a self-ruffle. Borders do increase the cost of the window treatment, however. Tiebacks can be made of fabric, cord, ribbon, braid, yarn, or hemp. You need a generous scoop for them to be really pretty.

Hardware: Rods versus Poles

Rods, usually flat and made of white metal or plastic, are meant to be invisible. They can be curved to fit bay windows, and they are usually adjustable; you can fit them to your window without having to order an exact size. If you are going to open and close draperies daily, a traverse rod is almost a must. Its built-in track system allows you to open or close draperies using an attached cord or wand without pulling them off their pins or creating a disheveled appearance. Rods aren't particularly attractive. Cover them with a valance or cornice or ruffle.

Tension Rods. These are as basic as they come, and inexpensive. They are rubber tipped and come with a spring mechanism that holds them in place within the window frame. But tension rods tend to tilt or sag. Your curtains will always be lopsided if you frequently try to get access to the window or if the fabric is heavier than a lightweight muslin, linen, or lace.

Poles. Poles are round and usually made of wood or metal, in diameters from 1 to 5 inches. After a decade of fat, fatter, and fattest poles, we've swung back to skinny iron ones. Now a lovely 1- or 2-inch pole seems just right for all but the heaviest curtains. Simple curtains and window treatments without headers or outer curtains should always hang from poles, not rods. Poles are visible and should be decorative, though simple in style.

An attractive wooden pole is part of the window's decoration.

Finials. The caps on the ends of the pole that keep the curtains from falling off come in many sizes and shapes. My advice: don't get cute. A customer recently said she wanted something whimsical, such as frog-shaped finials. I prefer a simple ball or a classic motif.

If you have a painted-wooden rod with wooden rings and you are going to open and close the curtains regularly, you will scratch the paint. This happens on some less-expensive metal poles, as well. Use rods instead.

Ball Finial

Keep in mind the placement of your curtain, swag, or valance as you plan where to install hardware brackets. For very long windows, you will need multiple brackets along the pole, not just at the ends, or the poles will sag and droop.

SHADES

A shade is a window treatment that can be raised or lowered by means of a spring mechanism or cording system. There are a great range of styles, fabrics, and materials from which to choose. Depending upon your needs and the look you're after, you can use most shades alone on a window or paired with another treatment. Some shades are light-filtering and provide sun protection during the day. Types that are popular include balloon shades, Austrian shades, Roman shades, the simple roller shade, and pleated or cellular shades.

Balloon Shades and Austrian Shades

Always made of fabric, balloon shades and Austrian shades are often confused with one another. A *balloon shade* is gathered and scalloped and hangs flat until the bottom, where all the fabric is gathered. When you pull the cord to raise the shade, the fabric bunches up into soft folds. If you completely unroll a balloon shade, the fabric will lie flat. (See the illustration on page 115.) That's why a balloon shade is best as a stationary treatment. An *Austrian shade* has the full-

An inside-mounted balloon shade reveals handsome window trimwork.

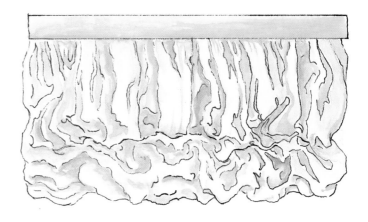

Balloon Shade

Austrian Shade

ness distributed throughout its length because the fabric is sewn into gathers, somewhat like smocking. The full fabric length is double the drop of the shade. If you completely lower an Austrian shade, it will still fall into

The scalloped edge lines up with the muntins.

multiple gathered folds. Often made of sheer or lacy fabric, an Austrian shade can be used alone or as an under curtain for heavy draperies.

Too often balloon shades are made of the wrong fabric. Ordinary cottons just don't look right. You need a silky fabric such as taffeta to get the crinoline-like desired effect. Also, people add too many embellishments—bows, fringe, and trim—to a design that is already a bit frivolous. For the best look, when the shade is installed, the scallops along the bottom should line up with the window muntins and the repeat in the fabric if it is prominent. (See the illustration above.) Some styles can have tails, too. By omitting the side cords on a balloon shade, you create a tail on each end. Tails can drop a few inches

or double the width of the scallop. Shorter tails look better when there are multiple scoops.

Roman Shades

Roman shades are flat fabric shades that pull up into neat, wide folds. Roman shades are richer and fuller than roller shades but still what I would call a minimalist window treatment. They have an architectural look and work best with solid fabrics or simple patterns such as stripes. A large-repeat pattern looks awful as a Roman shade because there is no softness in the overall appearance. Because Roman shades don't require a lot of fabric, you can afford to splurge and spend more per yard.

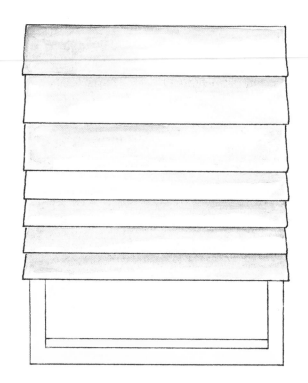

Roman Shade

There are other simple fabric-panel shades with a rod pocket at the top and fabric ties—you just roll up the shade and fasten the ties by hand at the bottom—a good do-it-yourself project.

Roller Shades

Roller shades are basic, but classic. I recently noticed that Calvin Klein has black ones in his house in the Hamptons. Look for roller shades that are constructed of a tightly woven fabric treated with a stiffening agent, a standard available option. I like roller shades with the round, white crocheted pulls that grandma's shades had. Alone, a roller shade is a simple, almost austere treatment that

Roller Shade

works if you are an all-or-nothing person. When the shade is up, there is nothing covering the window; when it's down, there is no view. Some roller shades can be bottom-mounted to conceal the lower portion of the window while allowing light to enter at the top—a great option for privacy in the city.

Pleated and Cellular Shades

Pleated shades are a soft alternative to blinds. They are made of permanently folded paper or fabric. Cellular shades are made of two or more layers of folded fabric, which create three-dimensional "honeycomb" cells. They have all sorts of options for translucency, light and heat

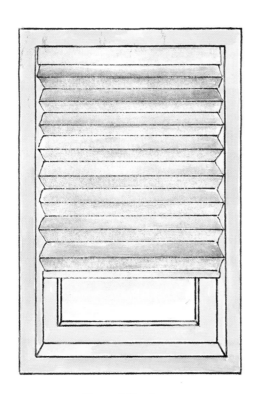

Pleated Shade

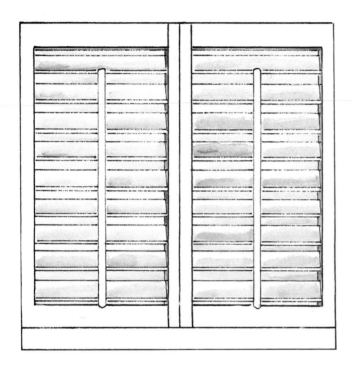

Plantation Shutters

Venetian Blinds

insulation, and UV protection, and they stack to a very thin sliver of fabric. However, I don't think they're especially pretty.

Shutters and Blinds

Shutters and blinds offer the ability to control and direct light and maintain privacy. Their louvers or slats can be manipulated to bounce light off the ceiling rather than the computer screen. (And a white ceiling will reflect more light back into the room.) Both treatments look best mounted inside the window frame. Shutters can be slightly or completely opened. However, they do block some light (albeit a lesser amount) even when their slats are opened all the way.

Because blinds have less hardware than shutters, they block less light. Wide-slatted wooden *plantation blinds*, otherwise known as old-fashioned venetian blinds, are currently the rage and with good reason—they are practical and attractive. Use ones with 2-inch-wide slats; although wider slats are available, they look exaggerated on most windows. Also be aware when choosing plantation blinds that the heading from which they hang is almost 3 inches deep. If you're looking for a nice, sleek installation, and you don't have very deep window recesses, the box will project out from the window frame and detract from the look. When you raise the blinds, wide slats can look like a

Shutters with wide, adjustable louvers are good looking and practical.

Matchstick Shade

A simple **blind** looks understated and elegant here.

stack of wood. (Raising a 36-inch-long blind yields a bulky "block" of wood at the top.) It's better to use these blinds where you want to manipulate the louvers and raise the blind for air circulation. Thin metal or plastic blinds, on the other hand, stack very compactly. *Miniblinds* (with $1/2$-inch-wide slats) don't offer total light blackout, but they are perhaps the least expensive option other than basic roller shades. They do control and direct light and offer a good degree of privacy.

The header section of blinds may protrude slightly.

Similarly, with *bamboo* and *matchstick blinds,* the larger the size and weight of the straw, the bulkier the blind when you raise it, as my client, Susan, and I just discovered. We ordered a wonderful natural-looking bamboo blind, but when we raised the thing, it looked as thick as a log. On the other hand, matchstick blinds give you a less bulky alternative. Typically, they are light-filtering during the day and offer partial privacy at night.

GETTING THE HANG OF WINDOW TREATMENTS

The late great American decorator, Billy Baldwin, was once working for a very rich man who declared that you could judge someone's wealth by the length of the

Sill length

Apron length

Full length

curtains, and the curtains Baldwin had recently designed for him were too short! "Then sir, your drapes will come down the wall, across the room, through the hall, and out the front door. As will I," replied the exasperated decorator. For me there are only three curtain lengths to consider: sill, apron, or full length. I prefer full-length curtains unless the window is tiny. On a small, ordinary window, sill length or apron length is a good choice because it will hide some of the sill and the apron below the curtain, giving a cleaner look to the overall design and adding greater visual size to the window. Then of course we have *puddled curtains*, which is a term that

Puddled curtains
pool slightly on
the floor.

These panels skim
the bookcase
below the
windowsill.

"For adequate fullness, generally curtains should

refers to curtains that are floor length and then some—puddled curtains have an extra allowance of at least 6 to 8 inches of fabric at the hem that allows a soft "puddle" on the floor.

The question of how long to make a valance or a fixed balloon curtain is more perplexing. You'd think that placing it below the trim at the top of the window would be just right. But because, for the most part, you are looking up at the tops of windows, you have to come down a few inches or everything under the valance will be visible—the storm window, screen, roller shade hardware, or blind header. When deciding how long to make a valance, go with a length that will place the valance a few inches lower than the bottom of the top trim of the window and the curtain hardware.

Rod Placement

I think a good rule of thumb is to install curtain rods equidistant from the top of the window molding to the bottom of the ceiling molding (or the ceiling line if you don't have molding). To maximize light, mount poles outside the window frame so that the curtains cover the wood trim (if there is any), but leave the glass exposed. If the poles or rods hang on the window frame, it is hard to push the curtains to the side, and they crowd the face of the glass.

How To Measure

You can spend a month or two waiting for the fabricator (in the case of curtains) or the installer (in the case of blinds or shutters), or you can learn to measure yourself and expedite the process. Maybe the fabricator won't start to sew until he or she has field-measured. (That means at your home or wherever the curtain is to hang.) But based on your measurements, he or she should be able to estimate the price and yardage requirements, provided you have taken careful and thorough measurements. That way you can decide whether you can afford new window treatments and go ahead and order the fabric. For adequate fullness, generally curtains should be *at least* two times the width of the window. If a window is 4 feet wide, then I recommend about 10 linear feet of fabric. I always tell my fabricators that I would rather err on the side of too little than too much—usually I just do twice the width of the window.

Two Things to Know When Measuring. First, yardsticks are an accident waiting to happen. They have numbers on both sides, not just in front and on the back, but on the left and right edges of the same side. The problem is that the numbers run down from 1 inch to 36 inches on the right edge and then from 36 inches to 1 inch on the left edge. Very confusing and very easy to make a mistake. I don't recommend a soft measuring tape, either. The final

be at least two times the width of the window. "

measurement can vary by how tautly you stretch the tape. Another common blunder is transposing length and width. Last week a decorating editor and her photographer husband told me they had done that and ended up with a really short, really wide window blind. Sometimes people just record the numbers without noting the width or length. They get to the store and can't remember which is which. All window treatment manufacturers' order sheets put width first and length second. Why not play it safe and follow suit?

Use a Retractable Metal Measuring Tape. Also, have a pen and a pad on hand and, if the window is wider than

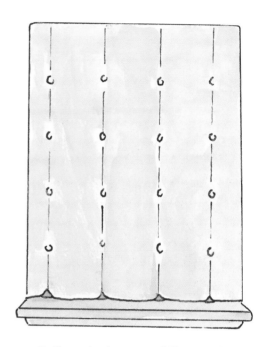

Balloon shade resting fully extended

*Hang the curtain rod equidistant
between window and ceiling molding.*

your outstretched arms, a helper to hold the other end of the tape. In my house, I measure; my husband installs. Blinds and shades are usually *inside-mounted* (inside the window frame), so measure the width of the window in several spots in case your windows are out of square, as mine are. You need only to measure the length in one spot. The length is not as sensitive as the width because the blind or shade can rest on the sill when it is fully extended. (See the illustration, above.)

I tend to hang hardware for curtains, which are usually *outside-mounted* (outside the window frame), equidistant between the window trim and the crown molding or ceiling line. The finials should extend about 6 to 8 inches outside the trim. If you intend to close the curtains, measure the width from bracket to bracket, and add at least 3 inches for a center overlap. Then, decide where you want the bottom of the curtain to fall (sill, apron, or floor). Measure down to that spot from the bottom of the rod or pole. If the curtain will hang from rings, measure from the base of the rings *after* they are installed on the rod or pole. Remember that the pin pulls the curtain up a bit, so allow an extra $1/2$ inch when measuring from the bottom of the ring. You won't be able to fix a too-short curtain, so when in doubt, make the curtain a little longer. And for a puddled effect, you can add another 3 to 6 inches.

MATCHING THE TREATMENT TO THE WINDOWS

Just as with apparel on the body, some styles look better than others. For example, dormer windows project out from attic rooms, usually from a sloped roof. They're typically located in a tight space and don't let in a lot of light because they are recessed into walls. Keep window treatments light and airy and simple. You can either fix the rod on the sides of the dormer or, if low light is a problem, install bracket-style rods that swing out and lay flat. (See the illustration, right.)

Palladian-style, or arched, windows or doors usually consist of a center unit flanked by two narrower units.

(See the illustration on the next page, top left.) The center window is topped with a half-round unit. Sometimes all three units are topped by one fanlight-style arch. I find these difficult to treat, and I'm not really crazy about any solution. It's usually better to treat the top half-round separately from the bottom. The top treatment should be stationary or even fixed, if you must cover it. The bottom treatment should be operable. If privacy is not an issue, a fixed balloon shade can be a beautiful solution.

Bay windows comprise several separate units, but you should treat them as one window for the greatest success. You have two choices: hang curtains at the intersection of each window, or hang them only at the two outermost ends. (See the illustration on the next page, top right.)

Dormer Window Solution

Palladian-Style Door Solution

Bay Window Solution

Roman or balloon shades or shutters on each individual window are also good solutions.

French doors can open outward or inward. If they open inward, as mine do, curtains mounted on a wooden pole or traverse rod above the doors must extend beyond the door trim. (See the illustration, right.) Vertical blinds are all wrong on French doors, but door-mounted horizontal blinds or roller shades, or even curtains of a thin material such as lace or linen, work fine.

Casement windows are vertically hinged and operate with a crank. Most of them swing out, but a few swing in.

French Door Solution

Casement Window Solution

Narrow Window Solution

That means you need a treatment that won't interfere with the window's operation. Having the crank at the sill means that shutters are a big no-no. Blinds should sit about 3 inches above the crank, or they will be lopsided at the bottom. The same is true for a permanent Roman shade. The bottom of the shade cannot rest on the sill, so it should be about 3 inches above the crank. If that arrangement is not a light or privacy problem for you, blinds and romans are fine. Soft window treatments, such as curtains, soft Roman shades, and soft balloon shades, which have some give and will drape over the crank, are by far your best bet. (See the illustration, left.)

Double-hung, or sash, windows, which go up and down vertically, are the most common window style and have barely changed in 200 years. They are easy to please and go with virtually any and every style of window treatment.

Camouflaging Flaws, Emphasizing Attributes

Small windows demand simple window treatments—no elaborate swags or festoons here. Make them seem bigger, taller, or wider by hanging the curtain outside the window frame. If this is not the desired effect, use a simple sill-length curtain. The elaborateness of the balloon doesn't work well on a small window; the divine simplicity of the Roman shade or a simple roller shade is better. If the window is narrow, simply extend the rod and curtain beyond the width of the window. (See the illustra-

A window treatment should never interfere with the operation of a window or door.

Roller shades provide adjustable light control in this bedroom.

An Austrian shade, mounted inside the frame, enhances this shapely window.

tion on page 118.) If it's a short wide window, make the curtains longer than the window frame—at least a few inches below the sill, if not floor length. On a stair landing, a graceful window treatment will draw attention.

If you have an ugly window that you have to live with, you should make the dressing subtle, quiet, and understated. The less attention you draw to it the better. However, if you are blessed with a beautiful view, play it up. Choose curtains that blend into the wall color—that way, what's outside the window can be the star.

More Window Treatment Wisdom

- ▶ Watch out for radiators: curtains hanging in front of radiators will block heat and eventually rot and discolor. Installed in front of an air conditioner or vent, they will impede the flow of cool air.

- ▶ If you're mounting blinds on a door with a handle, put the controls opposite the doorknob. You may need hold-down brackets.

- ▶ Curtains, like a new hairstyle, must be trained. Tease the folds into place; then pull the curtains and secure them with tape or a small piece of twine. Leave them alone for a few days; then set them free.

- ▶ Eventually you will want to clean your curtains. If the fabric has not been treated to resist shrinkage, wash it before the curtains are made.

- ▶ When hanging a curtain on a rod, drape the curtain over your shoulder so it doesn't slip down the rod or the eye pins aren't pulled out of the rod. Do the same when you wash or re-hang curtains.

CHAPTER 5

FURNITURE

Repeatedly, I am asked how the Internet will affect my world, **the home furnishings world**. Will we buy our sofas and sectionals online? I don't think so. Purchasing a sofa is not like buying books or music. Usually we work up to acquiring a major piece of furniture after months of **deliberation and budget debates** with our spouses. **How many sofas** will we buy in our lives? Maybe six or seven at most but probably not even that many. A good sofa can outlast a marriage—even a lifetime. Time put into the front end of **furniture selection is paid back infinitely** over the life of your family. And if you have chosen well, the furniture remains for other generations to enjoy. Do we need to visit the store to actually see and sit on the sofas and chairs and to **examine the table or chest**? I believe we do.

When it comes to furniture, quality and detail are important, not quantity and excess. To add warmth and personality to your home, I recommend both new and vintage pieces.

A plump club chair and ottoman are perfect for reading or napping.

The way I think we will use the Web in the home furnishings area is as a search engine. These Web sites are great for educating us as to what is available at what price and at directing us to the right stores. Maybe after we have visited the right store, we will order via a *dot com* company. Online, in a catalog, or in person, when selecting a sofa or chair, the criteria for determining quality and durability are the same: frame, construction, springs, cushioning, and fabric. When purchasing something with which you will interact physically, it is preferable to test it out. There are so many variables: height, pitch, pillow content, leg style, arm shape, loose cushion or tight back, seat depth, skirted or platform, tailored or pleated, foam or down — let alone hard or soft. Just how interactive is that Web site?

UPHOLSTERED FURNITURE

You cannot know how a sofa or chair will seat you unless you actually sit on it. Where will the front of the seat intersect with your thighs? How will the frame cup your back? Will the arms be just the right height for supporting your elbows when you are reading *Vogue* or for dad to hoist himself into an upright position? Will the seat be wide enough to squiggle and squirm in when reading to a child or snuggling up with a book? Will it be narrow enough to support your back if it is an upright chair? If it is a sofa or a sectional upon which you will be reclining, then stretch out on it. Don't be embarrassed. If you're looking for a sofa on which to recline at home, recline on it in the store. This is the only sure way to find out whether it is proportioned to your body.

Tailored to You

A friend of mine bought a straight, high-armed sofa that not only made her feel claustrophobic when reading but was impossible to stretch out on. The arm was too high to rest her head on, and the body was too short for her to be entirely stretched out. It was an attractive piece of sculpture, not a cozy napping or relaxing sofa. For the napping position, you need a nice round dropped rolled arm for your head, such as the one on the sofa pictured on page 135 of this chapter.

Another friend, Kim, commented to me that a lot of today's furniture is only comfortable for lying down, that it's too deep for comfortable sitting. As Kim's condo has a combination living/family room, that is a problem for her. In the living room — if you have a separate living room — those pieces of sculpture that we call furniture are often meant to be looked at instead of sat in. Conversely, in the family room, the furniture rarely gets a day off.

As a short-legged, long-waisted creature, I like a chair that is low to the floor and has a high back. My neck is worn out at night, and I love the luxury of leaning back and having my neck supported. I also like a chair with arms that support my elbows while I am reading, and I like a sofa that is fairly low so I can stretch out on it. On the other hand, if the seat is too low, I have to heave myself to an upright position — sort of rock myself up in order to exit. My father rocks himself forward to attain a vertical position, and it's not a pretty sight. If you're long-legged and seated in a low-slung chair, your knees will be up to your chin.

Sizing Up Seating

Here are some numbers to add comfort to your life: a seat height of 15 inches is low to the ground. You will literally drop into this chair; 19 inches is high, the usual seat height of a wing chair, which by nature has a springy,

A tag-sale treasure, this high-back chair supports my neck.

The straight-forward design of the banker's chair promotes good posture.

firm cushion. Older people tend to love wing chairs. The height plus an 18-inch depth make them easy in and easy out, with good arm leverage.

Seat Width. A chair seat should be 18 to 24 inches wide. Anything narrower, and you'll feel fenced in. That luxurious club chair with the 15-inch-high seat should be deep, too — approximately 22 inches deep (from the front face of the seat cushion to the front face of the back or back cushion). Remember that low and deep require effort to get out of the chair. If a chair seat narrows toward the back, it provides better lumbar support than others, often the case with a wing

A wing chair, left, is easier to get out of than the heavily cushioned pieces, below.

chair. The slant of a chair's back is also crucial. It can throw you way back practically to the point of whiplash. If your chairs are for conversation rather than for resting, your guests will be seated with necks straining as they lean forward to chat.

Standard Sofas. Most standard sofa frames are designed to accommodate a sofa bed, whether they contain one or not. It is a form of inventory control—fewer frames to house at the factory. Thus, standard sofas measure 68 inches between the arms that may be 6, 7, or 8 inches wide. Depending on arm width, other standard sofa widths may be 80, 84, or 88 inches. Don't think you are getting more seating with the longer length. As the frames are typically a fixed size, all you're getting is more arm. Sofas come in few sizes because most manufacturers have only a couple of standard frame sizes. In my opinion the 68-inch interior seat length is too skimpy for the family room. It dates from the days before big-screen TVs, remote controls, and videos.

If two of you want to be comfortable, add an ottoman to your sofa seating. That way you can both stretch out. (Ottomans are not just for chairs, and they can double as coffee tables.) Like marriage, buying a sofa calls for compromise. One size does not fit all family members equally. When determining the length of the sofa, obviously family size counts, too. Our family room sofa is

Ottomans on wheels expand a room's seating options.

custom-made, and we are crowded. A 38- to 39-inch depth is comfortable for both sitting and reclining.

If you are buying seating, consider a pair of his and hers chairs. They can have identical proportions, except for the depth (women's legs are generally shorter). From the front, when they are lined up, the difference in depth is not appreciably visible. In an upstairs TV room that I designed for a couple in Connecticut, his and hers chairs

Different chair proportions suit different individuals.

are paired with ottomans. The couple report that they heave a mutual sigh of contentment when they settle into their chairs at the end of a long day. The message: buy seating that suits your body and the bodies of your family —and the needs of a room. One for baby bear, one for grandpa bear, and one that's just right for you!

The Inside Story

Decided on the look, the style, and the shape? There's more! Now it's on to the insides of the sofa or upholstered chair. After you've invested time, money, and anxiety over price, comfort, and look, you want your purchase to last. Quality and durability are determined by the frame and construction, springs, cushioning, and fabric.

SOFA
SIGHT LINES

When selecting a sofa that won't be pushed against a wall, check the back and sides for an attractive profile. My living room sofas are viewed from the side as I enter and leave the room. Although they are seldom used, they are seen constantly, and their profiles are important to me. Freestanding, floating in the room, flanking the fireplace, their high tight camelbacks give them interest and visual appeal. My living room sofas are also about style and fabric and shape, whereas my family room sectional, with soft, rounded, rolled arms, is all about cushioning, comfort, and cozying up.

The Frame. Sit on the arm of a sofa or chair: you shouldn't be able to feel any evidence of the wood frame inside. The frame is frequently referred to as the skeleton of the furniture; this is where quality begins. Most pieces of new good-quality furniture have frames made of kiln-dried hardwoods, commonly maple and oak, which offer both strength and resilience. Inexpensive substitutes, which include plastic, metal, plywood, particleboard, and other manufactured materials, do not make durable furniture frames. Ever sit on a sofa or a chair with a wobbly or lopsided frame? Using kiln-dried hardwoods ensures that the frame won't absorb moisture and will remain completely stable, without warping.

Springs and Cushions. Springs support the cushioning. They help determine how the piece sits and how it will hold up over time. Springs come in two basic forms: *round coils*, like traditional mattress coils; and flat, *S-shaped wires*. Individual steel coils should be connected to each other with twine. The industry standard of good quality is eight-way hand-tied springs. All coils or wires should have 8-gauge thickness; if not, they will stretch out over time, and the seating will become saggy.

The content of seating cushions and pillows has significant impact on both comfort and durability. Cushioning is the key element affecting the way upholstered seating feels. Cushions can be *loose* or *attached*. Foam cushions are designed to literally cushion the weight of the person sitting and to spring back when the person stands up. There are many different grades of foam. You want high-density white foam with a channeled-down wrap for the seat. Test the quality of the cushion by lifting it. A 2x2-foot cushion should weigh no more than 2 pounds.

Cushion Content

The down wrap, which must be channeled to distribute evenly and keep in place the cloud-like down, gives the cushion its "crown" and soft feel. All down-encased cushions are deluxe cushions. A good ratio is 80 percent down and 20 percent feathers. Down-wrapped cushions maintain their shape longer; they do not flatten and crush as much as plain foam cushions. Usually cushions are narrower and shorter at the front edge, then crown in the middle. The down contributes to the pillowy look and feel.

The down wrap is the "crowning touch" on these cushions.

A perfect blend. Never buy a sofa that uses foam for the back cushions. The back cushion should be a blend of 75 percent feathers and 25 percent down. As to all the die-hards who say there is nothing like the luxury of 100 percent down, I say Ha! Not only can allergies be a concern, but 100-percent down cushions flatten, lose their shape, and do not supply enough support.

Maintenance. Down and feathers last forever and are maintained with infrequent, periodic steam cleaning. The feathers do escape, however. To

Cushions should be fuller in the middle and tapered slightly at the edges.

lessen or prevent leaks, choose *ticking* for the layer of fabric between the cushion and the surface fabric. Ticking is a strong tightly woven linen or cotton fabric used in upholstering and as a covering for mattresses and pillows. The tighter the ticking weave, the less leakage of feathers there will be.

Depending on the quality of the foam core, you will have to replace the cushion insert, which is the entire content inside your fabric, in 5 to 10 years. If you rotate your cushions periodically, you will get 10 years of use. Generally the cushions in the center get the least use. But even the

end cushions usually occupy a preferred corner and a secondary corner.

The Many Shapes of Upholstered Style

Cushions, arms, and even legs have shapes that determine a sofa's style. Cushions and arms can be rounded or square. Legs may be bun style, twisted, turned, pyramid shaped, or upholstered. Even the base of the sofa has significance: platform or with skirt, pleated, gathered or straight? A full-front skirt descending in a single section from underneath the sofa cushion is the current favorite. It is clean-lined,

Pyramid-shape exposed legs look sleek and contemporary.

THE CUSTOM OPTION

If you want to change the size or proportions of your seating, you probably will have to go to a custom sofa, which is not as expensive as you might think. Even your local upholsterer will make you a sofa. Why not ask? However, ready-made seating has options. Standard options or upgrades might be cushion content or details such as piping on the arms or pleating on the skirt. Inquire. Unless a sofa is the special of the month and you're buying it off the floor "as is," you always have options. When you buy, be sure to have your salesperson put in writing the frame quality, spring quality, and cushion content you have ordered.

A ruffled skirt adds
country charm to this sofa.

eliminating a grandmotherly seam on the front apron of the seating. These small details are what save your sofa from being bland and basic. They also engender long-term love. And, if you love it, you will always be happy with your purchase.

Cushion Shapes

There are three basic shapes for cushions: T-cushions, of which there are two variations—squared-off and round-shouldered; tuxedo, or box, cushions; and Turkish cushions. (See the illustrations at right.)

- **T-cushions.** The name originated with the T-shape pillow that sat on a chair seat—a central cushion with little wings that wrap around a recessed arm. For a traditional sofa, the shape should be the slightly rounded version.

- **Tuxedo cushions.** Tuxedo, or box, cushions have a contemporary look—boxy.

- **Turkish cushions.** Think harem, think formal, think old-fashioned. That's Turkish.

Each of the pillow shapes has pros and cons. The T-cushion deceives the eye by making a large piece of furniture look smaller, which can be important in achieving proper proportion in a room. It breaks up the visual volume of the sofa frame. So if you are stuffing a lot

of sofa into a small space, consider the T-cushion. As for T-cushions on a chair, this style on the back gives better support to the shoulders than do square tuxedo cushions. The T-cushion not only hides the bit of back frame that is exposed with a tuxedo, or box, cushion but

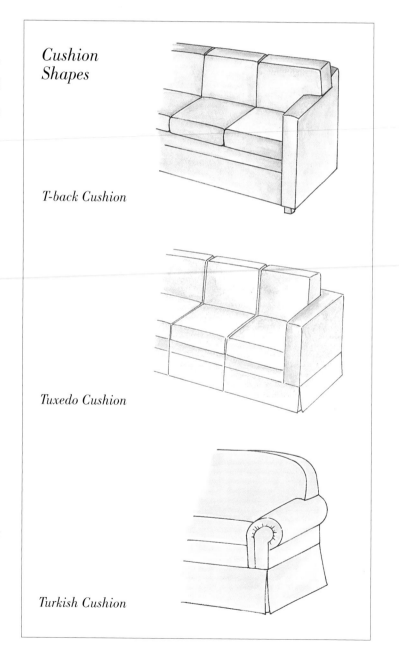

Cushion Shapes

T-back Cushion

Tuxedo Cushion

Turkish Cushion

supports the outside shoulder. The downside of T-cushions is, because of the definite corners, they are harder to rotate. The middle cushion is always the middle cushion. Additionally, as the T requires a recessed arm, T-cushioned seating is a bit harder to get into and out of. You don't have quite as much leverage as the full-extension arm that accompanies a square-cushioned sofa.

What Arm Shape?

Rolled is the standard arm shape; then there is rolled with an inset panel. Rolled arms can be from 6 to 12 inches in diameter; 8 to 9 inches is normal. And even a 10-inch arm requires an inset panel to tame the size. Get a 7- or 8-inch arm on a sofa and an 8- or 9-inch arm on a sectional. Rolled arms can be either recessed or full depth.

The *Bridgewater* arm is the English arm that generally goes with the turned-wood tapered leg with a brass wheel. It is a tight, small, recessed arm, rounded on the inside and straight on the outside. It is always recessed and therefore requires a T-cushion. Usually the Bridgewater arm is on a tight-back chair and always with an exposed leg and a tight back.

The *tuxedo*, or straight arm, is a boxed-top, squared-off arm measuring from 4 to 7 inches in width. Considerably smaller in proportion than the rolled arm, the tuxedo arm does not take an inset panel. As the arm is slim, less

The rolled arm, above, is full depth. On this sofa, right, the arm is recessed.

seating is sacrificed to arm size—something to keep in mind if you're tight on space.

Fabrication

Let's face it, no matter how well constructed your sofa, chair, or ottoman is, you will never enjoy it unless you like the way it looks. Many of the determinants of quality that I have listed are basically hidden under wraps. We cannot scrutinize the frame or see the coils, and how would we know what gauge the coils are, even if we could see them? One visible way to ascertain quality is to examine the fabrication. How well does the fabric match? Do the seams line up in both the front and in the back? On the arms? Fabrics with recognizable motifs should be centered and must match on the sides as well. Are the seams well sewn? Will they hold up to the heavy-duty pushing and pulling of everyday use?

If upholstery is tailored nicely on the outside, it is more than likely made well on the inside, too. Examine the details. Skirts should be lined and weighted to hang straight. And extras such as welting, piping, or cording on seams are not only decorative gestures but will greatly increase the life of the fabric.

Piping. Piping or welting, a double-edge fabric inserted in a seam, organizes the cushion covers on a loose-cushion sofa or chair and defines the shape on a tight-back piece. It actually helps the cushion or pillow hold its

shape, keeping the cover from looking "baggy." Piping should always have a fabric insert—not plastic—as the plastic will crack and start to look scalloped over time. Although piping is the first thing to wear out on a sofa, its benefits far outweigh the wear factor. Tight-back seating, especially, requires and benefits from piping. Good bone structure and shape are important for tight-back furniture, and the upholstery should emphasize those features. As these pieces look best in understated patterns, you can't count on pattern to conceal bad lines and design flaws. In contrast, a loose-cushion sofa can have a dreadful shape, but splatter it with a summery floral slipcover, and the shape is barely noticeable. (Luckily, pattern hides a multitude of sins on a sloppy old sofa.)

Contrasting piping accentuates the pretty lines of this dainty slipper chair.

Tufting. Tufting involves using buttons to tie down upholstered fabric. Tufting works wonders in adding personality to an otherwise plain tight-back sofa or chair. Tufting is best done with solid fabrics because it creates folds in the material. Don't use tufting on a pattern that has a geometric repeat. We used a stripe for a client's tufted bedroom ottoman long ago. The stripe wobbled like a drunken sailor at every tufted button. Live and learn. Of course we recovered the ottoman in an overall floral that eliminated the wobbly effect. Traditionally, velvets and leathers have been favorite materials for tufting for a very good reason: their lack of pattern is actually enhanced by the ornamentation.

Tufted sofas make for hard sitting, however. They do not

Tufting and brass upholstery tacks add interest to this leather sofa.

FURNITURE FACE-LIFTS

Your sofas and chairs will inevitably be re-covered in the course of your lifetime. Skirts, hems, piping, and details can be changed easily, and so can functional features. Concealed legs can be replaced with casters or even rockers and swivels. You can add a turned-wood leg with a brass wheel or just a brass wheel to an existing piece. I have an English sofa that was just too short for easy sitting. I ordered four brass casters from my upholsterer's catalog, and now it is just the right height. All upholsterers have these catalogs; the products are available at no great expense. Sometimes you can find what you need at a local hardware store or home center.

take down filling because the down will lump and clump around the buttons, causing bulges and bumps. Tufts are also difficult to repair and replace—an important consideration if you have children.

Legs. To each decade there is a furniture foot. Bun-footed sofas are an old-fashioned, early 1980s look. Pyramid legs are today's modern choice, while turned-wooden legs with brass casters demonstrate an ongoing infatuation with cozy English style. Boxed and recessed legs, which are not visible, make a sofa appear to float. If you choose recessed legs, they have to be 2 to 3 inches

high if you want to vacuum underneath the piece. I prefer 1-inch recessed legs, which means I must have a zillion dust bunnies and jelly beans and chips under my sectional sofa. Hey, we flip it over once a year and clean underneath, whether it needs it or not.

Skirts. Of course, there's the skirted sofa or chair. Today's traditional skirt has an additional seam on the front face of the sofa that is about equidistant between the cushion bottom and the floor. The so-called waterfall skirt, which descends seamless and uninterrupted from the sofa deck beneath the cushion, is a lovely variation. I

By adding wheels to the legs, I made this a comfortable-height desk chair.

love the look of it, especially the absence of the additional and obtrusive seam.

Sectional Seating

Sectionals come in a wide variety of configurations. For sectional seating, you can buy as many or as few individual sections as you need. Individual sections can be arranged in different configurations as your needs change. As the number of individual pieces increases, so do the cost and fabric requirements. If you want maximum flexibility, a sectional may be for you. Although you'll pay more up front and for re-covering later, nothing gives greater assurance that you'll find a home for your

seating no matter the situation. My family room sectional is 25 years old. A portion resides in my oldest daughter's apartment. Another remains in my teenage son's lair. All portions still wear the original fabric, albeit they are due for re-covering. If you don't know where you will be living in a few years, armless single sections are best for you. Smaller individual pieces give maximum flexibility. With a sectional, you can add modules as your family grows. (See the illustrations, below left.)

Fabric Considerations. Avoid overblown patterns on sectionals, or you will be overpowered by the print. Avoid solids, too.

A tight-fitting slip-cover updates this high-back chair.

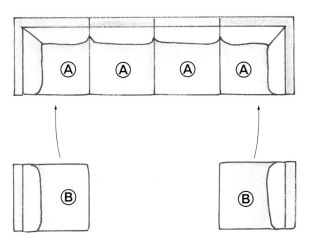

A miniprint or weave will deflect the eye and conceal both wear-and-tear and dirt and wrinkles. Prints should be subtle. A sectional takes 40 to 60 yards of fabric, whereas an average sofa requires 20 yards. The cost to re-cover is high, so you don't want to do it often.

Sectional Size. With anything beyond 40 inches deep, you'll find your feet may not touch the floor. The optimal depth is 38 to 39 inches from front to back, which is incidentally the size of a twin bed. (See the illustration below.) Remove the back cushions, and you've got an instant guest bedroom. "Mom, can we sleep in the TV room?" They know the answer, so why do they ask? Will it fit? Don't forget, with a sofa or a sectional, either the height or the depth must be narrower than the width of your doorways.

Sectional seating is versatile. Add pieces as you need them.

Customizing. When planning a custom sectional, keep all the cushions the same size. This will allow you to rotate them, minimizing wear. If you have 27-inch cushions on one flank and 25-inch ones on the other, confusion will reign when you remove the cushions to vacuum the sofa and then try to put cushions back again.

Like other sofas, sectionals can have dressmaker details like piping, a skirt, and pleats. Unlike other sofas, their individual sections can roll apart when you sit down. To prevent this, tie the legs together with picture wire.

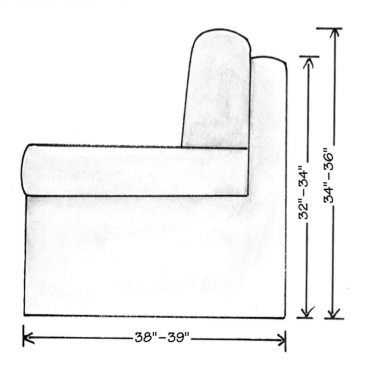

SLIPCOVERS

Slipcovers consume the same quantity of yardage that upholstery does but require less labor. Therefore, the labor cost is less. Despite the "shabby chic" mania of the past few years, slipcovers are not appropriate for every situation.

I have slipcovers in my living room. And they are tight, tacked-down slipcovers at that. Yet even in this seldom-used room, the fabric hikes up in the back. My advice is, where the cost-saving value of slipcovers is important, use them in a guest room, on a chair in a child's room that is just there to collect clothes, or on a seldom-used piece of furniture.

ASSESSING ANTIQUES

A home that's decorated only with new furniture can appear cold. Adding an antique or two does not mean you are committed to all antiques, nor does it rule out a contemporary interior. Antiques bring something unique and a part of history into a home. I love the added charm of antiques. The past lives of my furniture intrigue me and increase its appeal. I enjoy thinking about the lives before mine that have touched my furniture. Who sat in this chair? Whose face was reflected in this mirror? Antiques may offer other value, too. For example, my friend Sheree recently showed me a pine secretary she purchased 10 years earlier for $1,200. She was going to give it away. Instead we put it in an antique shop on consignment and sold it for $1,900. That's a pretty good return on an investment she'd owned for only 10 years. As we go through life, our tastes change and mature. Sheree no longer wanted a piece of rustic pine in her bedroom, preferring painted white furnishings. She made her new purchase without spending a thing thanks to the handsome profit on her pine piece.

By all means, buy an antique that tugs on your heartstrings, not your purse strings. But don't overlook the value of a piece, either.

Shopping Tips. Buy what you like. Going for the best value should always be secondary. If you are only interested in investments, go to the stock market, not the antique store. With antiques, look for pieces that speak to you. If a piece appreciates over time, it's an extra, a bonus. What really counts is how much you enjoy owning it and having it in your home. If you derive pleasure every time you walk by your Sheraton chair or use your farmhouse table, then it was worth buying. However, as with any investment, beware. There are an awful lot of fakes out there. It is important to do business with a reputable dealer. Examine the piece (or at least pretend to), and ask about specifics.

Many people don't seem to grasp the concept of an antique. Technically, a piece becomes officially antique at age 100. Anything old but under 100 is vintage. At this point, virtually every period from ancient to relatively recent has been rediscovered. That includes not only the stuffy old English country look but the Danish modern, as well.

Look Beyond the Obvious

There are a few simple ways to help determine the age and quality of a piece of furniture. If the antique is of good quality and care has been taken, the interior will be as nicely finished as the exterior.

Look to see what kind of wood is inside, at the back of a piece, and on the bottom of the drawers. A chest of drawers with a hardwood interior is excellent. An armoire finished with satin wood or a good-quality piece of bird's-eye maple is usually superior to one finished inside with a secondary wood like pine. Also see if the interior wood is finished or raw. Another indicator of quality is the construction on the inside.

Grandmother's porch furniture has sentimental value for me.

Our old Swedish pine sofa
is a family heirloom.

Components (the drawers) of an antique chest are put together with dovetail joints, for example. Double-dowel (peg) joints are used to hold the chest's frame together.

How Authentic Is It? Ask the dealer whether a piece is an original or a reproduction. If it is said to be original, ask to have it stated so in writing. Also ask for what is called the provenance of your piece. The dealer may not have a lot of facts, but there should be some history available such as: "English, latter half of the nineteenth century." Keep a file with all your antiques' receipts and their provenances. Later, if you want to sell a piece, you will know what you paid and hopefully what you bought.

Blended Styles. It's perfectly okay to mix and match eras and finishes, as long as the pieces complement each other. No rustic pine with formal mahogany, but only in the strictest sense. Of course, in my living room, I do have pine mixed with mahogany—my early New York City ancestors' mahogany and my husband's Scandinavian ancestors' pine. However, the mahogany is only semi-formal, and the pine is not really rustic. The Swedish pine piece is a sofa. It used to sit in a light, airy passage in my old house between the living room and kitchen. Now it has to be in my formal living room to provide balance with the fireplace. It sits along the only wall in the house that's long enough to accommodate its size and presence.

As soon as the sofa was in its new place, it looked so . . . well, pine. First I stained it a darker color. Then I decided to dress it up. I was having a gold leaf moment and got true gold leaf sheaves and burnished them onto the sofa with a coin, making a lattice design on the sofa's back panel. After that, I discovered gold paint in a pot and added more decoration, using my eyeliner brush to apply it. Still, my Swedish sofa looked a bit flat and dull, so I decided it needed a finish to give it just the right patina of age.

My living room coffee table is a leaf from my grandmother's old mahogany dining table. I removed a portion of the pedestal base to attain the correct height. Always save the removed pieces, as you may be able to reuse them. The

Use what you have. In this case, the leaf from grandmother's dining room table became our coffee table.

ball legs to my daughter's old pine chest now support a footstool. I keep a box of old parts and pieces in the basement. When cutting down a coffee table, remember that, like hair and flower stems, you can always go shorter. I like coffee tables on the high side: 16 to 18 inches.

THE CASE FOR CASE GOODS

Whether you're buying a bureau, side table, dresser, armoire, buffet, or dining table, you are buying what in industry parlance is a *case good*. Case goods have no upholstery. Historically, furniture was made entirely from wood. Although always the correct choice, only 25 percent of all furniture today is solid wood; the rest is veneer. The term "solid wood" does not mean that one single piece of wood was used when building the piece, nor does it necessarily mean that all the wood throughout the piece is solid. Generally, the term means that all the exposed pieces of wood are solid; those unseen may be made of something else, such as plywood or particleboard.

Today for the most part, the top, sides, front, and back are wood, be it solid or veneer. Veneer is a thin sheet of wood that is laminated onto a plywood core. It is solid, sturdy, and light and not too expensive or heavy. If you want to tell the age of a piece of wood furniture, give it a lift. Solid wood is heavier than wood veneer. But particleboard is quite heavy, so it

This chest of drawers is a reproduction piece.

may be harder to tell than with pieces made with plywood.

The dining room buffet, made of cherry, is a French antique.

Check for Quality

The best quality furniture usually has dovetail joints (not ones that are glued, screwed, or nailed). The grains of these wood joints should match up. Lean on the table and tip back the chair. When buying a case good, be sure no cracks or bubbles are found in the finish. With a bureau, open the drawers and look inside. Rub your

A double-pedestal table seats
the most people.

hands along the sides and bottoms of the drawers. Are they smoothly sanded or rough and splintery? Will they snag your sweaters or tear your linens? Dresser drawers should open and close easily. Try and open the drawer with one hand only. Does it open smoothly and close firmly without jamming? Drawers should not wobble. Check that back panels are screwed and glued and not just stapled. Nails and screws make the back an integral part of the furniture. (Staples make the back something waiting to fall off.) Use this criteria to carefully scrutinize potential furniture purchases.

Examine Alignment. Quality furniture is made *square*. Check that drawers and doors sit well within their frames. Open doors and see how they hang. Do they sag on the frame or hang evenly and swing easily? A sagging door means that sooner or later it will no longer close properly. Door hardware should operate smoothly. Hinges should be strong and secure.

Step back, and take a long look at your piece. Does everything look aligned? Then turn the piece over and look underneath. Are there corner blocks to reinforce joints bearing weight? These corner blocks strengthen the joints and help ensure not only the stability of the piece but that it remains square.

There is no reason why a piece of fine wood furniture should not be handed down to your great-great-grandchildren. The way a piece of furniture is built will determine whether your descendants wind up with a treasured antique or a pile of kindling.

Table Talk

A dining room set is not going to be replaced. Typically, you buy only one. Get one that will fit the whole family, as it is now and how you expect it to grow. When testing a table, it is important to think about maximum seating, as well as individual seating comfort. Double-pedestal tables are very popular because they are classic in look and offer flexible seating around the perimeter, whereas a table with a leg at each corner limits seating.

When buying a new or old dining table, examine how it looks and how it sits. If you are like me, you are not comfortable unless your legs are crossed. A deep apron on an older table will mean no crossed legs. That may be okay for holiday meals but certainly not for everyday dining. However, if you have a deep-apron dining room table, you have an option. You can retrofit it. I had my carpenter reshape my formerly straight-apron table, adding a lovely curve to the corners. Now I can comfortably cross my legs and enjoy my time at the table.

"There is no reason why a piece of fine wood furniture shouldn't be handed down to your great-great-grandchildren."

The light finish helps these antique chairs mix well with less-formal styles.

Therefore, these narrow tables work better as sofa tables, hall tables, or even desks. Conversely, I recently dined at a table so wide that you had to walk around it to set the table. It was just too wide to reach over to the other side.

Room for More. If you don't have leaves for your table, you can have some made more easily than you think. Look in the Yellow Pages or the ads in your local newspaper for a cabinetmaker or a woodworker. My friend Michelle just had two made for her round ancestral claw-footed oak table. Now she can seat 16. A dining room table is for the most part a once-in-a-lifetime purchase. Be sure that it will do the job and carry you and your family through all the ages and stages of life. When your children get older, they move out, and when they come home there are more of them.

Before making your purchase, sit at the table and test it out. Be a method actor; think about how many you can seat, whether you will need placemats or tablecloths. With a finely finished piece, tablecloths and pads are a must. I recommend a light distressing. It is just so much more forgiving. (There I go again talking about high-stress interiors adding to high-stress lives.) How will you serve the food? Is there room for candles, serving platters, and water pitchers in the center of the table when the place settings are installed? Oftentimes older farmhouse tables or refectory tables are quite narrow.

Sets of dining room chairs go up exponentially with the number of chairs. A set of twelve will cost a lot more than a set of eight of equal quality. Not just 50 percent more. Eight will cost a lot more than a third more than a set of six. If you can't purchase all the chairs at one time, rather then getting six side and two armchairs, get all side chairs. You can always marry the eight side chairs with different armchairs down the road. Besides, it's interesting to mix the different

A slightly distressed tabletop is a practical choice.

styles and pieces. I wonder who in the world has my other armchair?

Whether you're buying old or new, antique, vintage, or right off the furniture-showroom floor, make purchase decisions with trepidation and proceed with caution, forearmed with knowledge. To be better informed, ask the upholsterer, the furniture salesman, and the antiques dealer. Too often we assume that we are only entitled to pull out our checkbooks and take the product home. Find out what you need to know first.

COORDINATING EXTRA CHAIRS

To give you additional seating flexibility, think about how your dining chairs look with your kitchen chairs before making a purchase. (I assume you won't have 16 dining chairs.) Mine look great together. They are essentially a similar Queen Anne style. The dining room chairs are finished in a light cherry, and the kitchen chairs have a burgundy finish, which looks great with the room's Oriental rug.

CHAPTER 6

LIGHTING

Lighting a home is not like buying a sensible pair of shoes. It's about **magic, sparkle, and the ability to transform**. No single element of design is as important as lighting. Without it there is no beauty. Of all inventions, **artificial lighting** is perhaps the most **eloquent**. From the electrified candle in the window to the fluorescent strip under the cabinets and the **chandelier** over the dining table, nothing is **more flattering**, **makes tasks easier**, and **sets a mood** better than good lighting. Unfortunately, discussions about lighting for the home are often too technical or simply incomplete. But they don't have to be. In this chapter, I'll explain all you really need to know about the **basic types of light**, why they're important, and how to address them. I'll also offer advice for **choosing the right combination** of lighting fixtures for your home.

Set the stage, brighten a dark corner, or make humdrum tasks easier by choosing the right bulbs and lighting fixtures for every room in your home.

LIGHTING WITH A PURPOSE

When you're watching TV award shows, have you ever noticed that performers look exceptionally lovely on stage, but when the camera pans them back in their seats, they look like me and thee? That's because the stage lights are intended to flatter them while the auditorium lights are meant for plain old general illumination. The two types of lighting are used to accomplish different things. In your home, you should use a combination of the three basic types: ambient (or general), task, and accent light for aesthetic as well as practical purposes.

Ambient Light

The word "ambient" means to go around or surround on all sides, and it's the term used for all-around illumination in a room. Ambient light is usually supplied from standard, ceiling-mounted fixtures, but it can come from recessed lights or wall sconces, too.

Ambient light may be necessary, but I don't think it has much *ambiance* at all. So when someone describes a room's ambient light, don't expect

Combine different fixtures to create interesting lighting effects.

anything special or even pleasing. Ambient light is just standard-fare general illumination.

Task Light

As the name implies, task light focuses on the task at hand. It illuminates the work surface, not the room. Metal architects' lamps are a perfect example. They do what they were designed to do very well: direct an intense beam of light onto a small surface. Other examples of task lights include under-cabinet kitchen lights, reading lamps, and desk lamps.

When designing or installing task lighting, it is important to think

An adjustable-arm lamp provides good task lighting.

about where your body will be in relation to the work surface and the light source. If you place yourself between them, you'll cast a shadow, which defeats the purpose. On the other hand, if you aim the light directly onto the work surface, you'll create glare.

Placement. Optimally, task lights should be angled between you and the work. A reading lamp is best when it comes over your shoulder, for example. In the bathroom, vanity lights should be on both sides of the mirror, not above it. I learned this early on when I noticed a difference in the way I looked in my sister's powder-room mirror compared with my own. There was a single overhead light over my mirror, and my reflection looked haggard at 25. But when I visited my sister's powder room, where there were side-by-side sconces flanking the mirror, I looked young and cute. My overhead light caused the upper portion of my head to cast shadows on the lower portions of my face. My brows shadowed my eye sockets. My nose shadowed my lips, my lips shadowed my chin, and so on. Get the picture? It was not a pretty one. Overhead lighting is certainly not for looking in the mirror—or for putting on makeup or grooming your hair. It's like the lighting in a department-store dressing room, unflattering.

Accent Light

Accent light is intended to show off or draw attention to something: the niche on the stair landing, the table at the end of a long hall, the art over the mantle. Accent light

usually needs to be angled, typically toward the object it's illuminating. When you want to highlight something special—an object, a photograph, a piano, or the fronds of a large potted plant, to name a few things—be sure the light source is concealed. It is the object and not the light source that we want to see.

ILLUMINATION AND ILLUSION

We need ample amounts of light for a lot of reasons. Besides brightening our world, light can visually manipulate space, making a room seem larger or smaller. Light can define activity zones in multifunctional rooms. It can show off desirable aspects of a room and the architecture while obscuring or distracting from less-attractive features. Light, or the lack of it, even alters mood. Seasonal Affective Disorder, which occurs in the winter when the days are short, is a state of depression brought on by diminished amounts of natural light.

You can control and manipulate light in several ways: the angle from which you direct it, the intensity, and the color. We know instinctively that we need one kind of light for walking down the hall, another for reading, yet another for food preparation in the kitchen, and still another at the computer screen. Although we know what we want, we don't always understand how to make it happen. A good place to begin a plan is choosing the proper light source.

Soft lighting enhances the drama of color and architecture.

Table lamps, like these, typically use incandescent bulbs.

Incandescent Bulbs

These are the regular rounded bulbs (the type Thomas Edison invented) that everyone knows. Initially, they are the least-expensive lighting option to buy (but not the most economical to use), and they are still the most universal form of residential lighting. They emanate a warm, cozy glow that accentuates reds and yellows in a

A pair of hanging pendants are ideal over a long table.

descent bulbs are not a good idea in a tight, confined space such as the interior of an airless desk unit or recessed under cabinets.

Take the case of my client Ed's New York City apartment, which had a closet that I converted into a home office for him. I was dead set against installing fluorescent fixtures because they are unattractive. Instead, I specified fixtures that use incandescent bulbs. However, the compact space got so hot that Ed had to turn the lights off altogether. Picture it: there's Ed, his office equipment, and the lights—all generating standing heat. The small space became an oven. Looking back we should have concealed some bright, long-lasting cool fluorescent strips under Ed's upper bookcase unit instead. No one would have seen the strips, and Ed wouldn't have had to choose between working in the dark and roasting.

Standard incandescent bulbs also lose their luster with age and burn out frequently. Fortunately, there are new, longer-lasting versions. Even though they're more expensive, these bulbs should be considered for a hard-to-reach area, such as a stairwell that is accessible only by a ladder. Our porch lantern is another such example. Without realizing it, we must leave the porch light on

decorating scheme and are generally flattering to you and your interiors.

What's bad about incandescent bulbs? They are inefficient, which is reflected in your energy bill. The burning filament inside an incandescent bulb emits light as a by-product of heat. Because 90 percent of the effort goes into generating heat rather than illumination, the bulb gets hot—sometimes dangerously so. That's why incan-

"there are new, longer-lasting versions . . . these bulbs should be considered for a hard-to-reach area, such as a stairwell . . ."

endlessly. The bulb always needs changing — so, out comes the ladder again.

Halogen Bulbs. Halogen is actually a type of low-voltage incandescent lamp. These bulbs run on just 12 volts of electricity and are smaller and more energy-efficient than other incandescent bulbs. A 50-watt halogen lamp provides as much illumination as a 75-watt standard incandescent bulb, for example. Halogen bulbs are not interchangeable with standard incandescent bulbs.

While they cost more, halogens burn longer, giving you more kilowatt hours for your dollar. So you might pay more for a halogen bulb, but you'll have to change it less frequently. The light is whiter than other types of bulbs and is more natural looking, too. However, halogens are hot and produce a lot of glare because the reflectors inside the bulbs intensify the light. Newer, low-voltage versions are brighter, compact, and more energy efficient.

Halogens come with screw-in or snap in-bases. Wear gloves or use a soft cloth when installing them. The oil from your skin interacts with the heat produced by the lit bulb, which will make the bulb smoke, give off a burning odor, and possibly explode. I recommend staying away from the older snap-in versions, which require expertise to properly install. Some halogen bulbs, the kind typically used in torchieres, can generate enough heat to burn your skin or start a fire if they're too close to flammable material.

Fluorescent Bulbs

Fluorescent bulbs give a lot of light. One 20-watt fluorescent bulb generates the same amount of brightness

Fluorescent strips fit easily under wall cabinets.

as one 75-watt incandescent bulb. That's a difference of almost four to one. Plus a fluorescent bulb lasts 10 times as long a standard incandescent bulb, so you won't need to replace it as often. Fluorescent light won't fade or diminish in intensity over time, either. No wonder these bulbs generate most of the light in the world today. Because the light they produce is cool, fluorescent bulbs are great for illuminating the kitchen countertop — you

> *" . . .you can save money lighting your home using the right bulbs and fixtures. "*

won't work up a sweat while chopping vegetables on a surface that already bears the heat from toaster ovens, coffeemakers, and other appliances. In addition, tube fluorescent bulbs can be quite narrow. Small, compact versions are ideal underneath wall-mounted cabinets. Larger ones work well in basements with low ceilings.

WHAT
DO YOU SAY
TO A NAKED BULB

The answer is lampshades. Just as linen and lace curtains diffuse light, *translucent* fabric lampshades diffuse or filter light while obscuring the naked bulb. On the other hand, *opaque* paper shades allow light to emerge solely from the openings at the top and bottom of the shade. They offer drama and will light whatever is underneath or above their circles of light, but they don't glow the way translucent shades do. One advantage of dark or opaque lampshades is that they will not reflect back at you from the windows at night or from the television screen.

If you want more-diffused light but really don't like translucent shades, the alternative is a paper shade with a gold lining. The soft reflection of the gold paper will enhance and increase the ambient light.

With so much going for them, why do fluorescent lights have such a bad reputation? Well, when you sit under one of them, you look like a laboratory specimen. Fluorescent light makes your skin color look awful, even ghoulish. Not pretty. The old standard types give a cool light that dulls those flattering, healthy, youthful red and yellow skin tones. Instead, they bring out blues and greens—colors that make you look sallow or seasick. Furthermore, light from fluorescent tubes cannot be directed or diffused. You can't dim most fluorescent light fixtures, and the bulbs hum when they need replacing.

Today's new choices in fluorescent bulbs are an improvement over the old standard type. They come in green, rose, and several shades of white, including cool white, warm white and a blue-white version. In addition to slim-line, miniature units, there are circular and compacted shapes. Considering the bang they give for the buck, I do champion their use in the right place.

If you still strongly dislike the look of any type of fluorescent bulb but want to illuminate your countertop or work surface, another option is a 25-watt incandescent lamp called a T-lamp or C-lamp, which looks like a string of tiny Christmas lights. However, these reflect back as a clutter of hot, bright-white dots over a shiny material such as marble or granite. Use them only in combina-tion with a matte-finished surface.

Period lighting fixtures enhance a home's style.

Wattage. I used to think that a low-watt bulb was just weaker than one with higher wattage, something like luke-warm versus hot water. But wattage isn't about the amount of light produced by a bulb, it's actually a measurement for the amount of electricity used to generate the light. According to some experts, on average lighting can consume as much as 15 percent of total household elec-tricity. That means you can save money lighting your home using the right bulbs and fixtures.

SETTING THE STAGE

Ever wonder why people comment about your carpet, the color of your walls, and your kitchen cabinets, but no one says anything about your lighting? Good lighting is perceived but not seen. Notice I didn't say it doesn't exist. I have a friend whose decorator has done a beautiful and expensive job of decorating her home. The textiles, furni-ture, and rugs are chic, practical, and perfect. Yet there is not a single light source in the room. In order to see this extraordinarily appointed interior, you have to look at it during the daytime. My friend says they are getting to the lighting next. Next? That's ridiculous. Skip a throw pillow or ottoman and buy a lamp! If you're on a budget, don't skip the lighting. Buy *some* of the new furniture and acces-sories and some of your lighting fixtures now; then add more things a little later.

How Much Is Enough?

When I entertain, my mother says all the lights in the upstairs rooms, including the attic, should be on so the house looks as warm and inviting as a candle in each window on a dark night. Let's not forget that this also makes the house appear larger when people approach it. On the main floor, set the stage with lots of lights, controlled with dimmers or by the correct wattage bulbs in lamps. One way to determine correct wattage is through a process of trial and error. Obviously, in rooms like the living room and the dining room where functions tend to be more leisure- and pleasure-oriented rather than task-related, a more subtle and subdued lighting is preferable. I use a combination of low-wattage light bulbs—nothing more than 60 watts each with overheads and sconces on dimmer switches. However, in the kitchen and family room, I need more task-specific and brighter light. For example, in the family room I rely on an overhead light also on a dimmer and three-way bulbs in my lamps with settings for removing splinters, reading, and napping. Be sure you check the lamp for the maximum wattage that is recommended before you load a 100-, 150-, or 200-watt bulb into it.

For every day, a good lighting scheme or overall plan will combine general lighting for background with specific task lighting, then touches of accent lighting for decoration. Ideally, all three sources will be on dimmer switches.

In any situation where a light will burn for long periods serving different functions and activities at various times of day, it's best to use a dimmer switch. My friend, Pat, said that when her friend, Ray, stayed in her apartment, he installed dimmer switches everywhere. Ray is a famous movie star's make-up man, so he knows the importance of good lighting. Although this is not a difficult job, you might consider calling in a licensed electrician if you have *any* qualms.

Dimmer switches, available in a few types, range in price from $6.50 to $150 and are found at any hardware store or home center. My advice is to keep it simple. You don't need anything expensive. The toggle switch with a sliding dimmer works for me.

Planning Your Lighting

Admittedly there are some general rules and a formula to determine how many watts of light to use for every square foot of space in your house. This never works for me. How many watts to do what? Walk? Read? Watch TV? For whom? Ten-year-old eyes can do practically anything in the dark. Fifty-year-old eyes are an entirely different story. Like all general rules of design, those that concern lighting can be broken. Ultimately, you will have to be the judge of what kind and how much light you need. The most important thing you can do with regard to lighting is to give it forethought.

Light Effects. Certain qualities about light are helpful to understand when you're devising a plan of action. For example, eyes are drawn to the brightest element in the room. Use this attraction to create visual tricks. At night a light in the garden can visually extend a room into the outdoors, for example. Also keep in mind that numerous lights are fine in a space that we pass through quickly, such as a hallway. But when we settle, the amount of light must be gentle. A room with dark walls will gobble up light, while a light-colored room will reflect and amplify it. So the darker the room, the more supplemental light you'll need.

Good reading light comes from behind over your shoulder.

Natural light. Designing artificial light is further complicated by natural light. Although sunlight is the most wonderful form of illumi-

An opaque lamp-shade softens light so there isn't glare.

nation, it's not like water from a tap that we can control just by turning it on and off. Furthermore, just because it's daytime doesn't mean you don't need extra light to illuminate a task. Weather conditions, how much sun comes through your windows, the color of the natural light all influence the supplemental light you'll need.

Address what you do and how you live in the room you are lighting. Act it out. Take notes. Do this for the big and little lighting decisions, including where to locate a switch. For example, if you're devising a lighting plan for

the kitchen, enter the room with groceries in your arms. Where does your hand naturally reach? Almost all rooms benefit from a centralized light source. A simple ceiling-mounted fixture made from milk glass or frosted glass will give uniform general illumination. Yet this type of lighting in areas where you spend extended periods of time is tiring to the eyes to say nothing of boring. How you plan to use the room will determine the amount and the type of lighting you will need.

LIGHTING TIPS FOR SPECIFIC ROOMS

I always marvel at the people who spend thousands of dollars to remodel a bath; then when they gaze into the bathroom mirror, they look like the cost of the job almost killed them. Actually, it isn't the price tag that makes them look terrible, it's the poor lighting. If only they had spent some of their budget on professional lighting advice. So here are some tried and true tricks-of-the-trade for lighting all through the house.

Kitchens

Any room is hard to light, but the kitchen is the greatest challenge. According to a survey conducted by architects, kitchens typically use 20 percent of the electricity for an entire house. There are more light sources in a kitchen than in any other room in the house, and they burn about 30 hours a week. That's longer than the TV is on and 50 percent longer than lights burn in other rooms.

A kitchen is divided into zones, each with its own lighting requirements. A laboratory and a family room, the modern kitchen has to accommodate diverse functions. A kitchen also contains shiny reflective surfaces and dark recesses. What's more, it can be dangerous anywhere there is the combination of electricity and water or fire and grease, slippery surfaces, and so forth. Food preparation and cleanup call for bright, shadow-free task lighting for good visibility. Use cool fluorescent bulbs for countertop illumination, and mount the fixtures right under the front edge of the upper cabinets. To minimize glare, choose a nonshiny countertop material. If the cabi-

nets don't have a strip to hide under-cabinet lights, add one. I installed decorative oak trim at the bottom of my wall-mounted cabinets to hide the fluorescent strip lights. To punch up the wattage over the sink, I recommend two 100-watt incandescent fixtures here or two 75-watt halogen lamps.

Beyond task lighting, the kitchen should have ample general illumination that is adjustable with a dimmer switch. Install recessed or ceiling-mounted fixtures approximately 12 to 15 inches from the front of the upper cabinets. That puts them roughly right over the outside edge of the countertop. This arrangement will sufficiently illuminate the interior of the upper cabinets when the doors are open as well as the front edge of the countertop or work surface.

Bathrooms

You need two kinds of lighting in the bathroom: ambient (general) light to get you to the shower or to take a pill, and a task light to tweeze your eyebrows and shave (or perform any other type of personal grooming).

To look good in a bathroom mirror, light should come at you horizontally from the sides. I gave my friend, Sara, some milk-glass shades for sconces in her master bath. She had the correct fixtures but the wrong shades. Hers were opaque rather than translucent. They

Sconces at both sides of a mirror are most-flattering.

allowed light to project only from the tops onto the ceiling. Dramatic? Yes! Functional? No. Her husband, Jerry, had to shave in the kids' bathroom where the task lighting was better. Shaving and applying makeup call for light that emanates from both sides of the mirror at eye level. The light should radiate from the middle of your face, usually about 60 to 66 inches high for adults. The right height may seem obvious, but I recently saw bathroom sconces that were almost 6 feet from the floor. The top of my head looked great.

Bulbs. Also remember that light generates heat. After a hot shower and the rush to get dressed, I can lean over the sink to put my contacts in and get soaked with dampness. I don't need a zillion watts of electricity for this final step, and neither do you. Choose bulbs that have enough power to produce a comfortable level of light without wilting you at the same time. To determine your comfort level, test out bulbs of various wattage until you find your level of preference.

Living Rooms

The ceiling represents 30 percent of a room's surface area, and large living rooms have lots of ceiling. Use it to both bounce light and contain sources of light. Ceiling lights break the hotel-lobby look of a flat, white ceiling and also raise the eye.

A hanging fixture in the center of the room creates balance and interest. So do recessed lights in the corners or near doors and windows. Floor outlets give additional flexibility for bringing in portable fixtures. If you have a full basement, installing an outlet in the floor is easy and inexpensive. A floor outlet will allow you to bring light into the middle of a

Modern pendants draw the eye to the far wall here.

edge of the table shines on guests' heads, laps or plates, casting unflattering beams and making everyone hot. Our body temperature rises anyway when we eat. To properly light the table, use a minimum of 150 watts and a maximum of 200 to 300 watts. Again, you may want to test this out to see what's comfortable for you. And don't forget to install a dimmer switch.

Good lighting in the dining room is second only to the food — OK, third to the company. However, if everything looks bad, everyone will be cranky and the food won't matter. When I had Thanksgiving with friends, I secretly reset the dining room lights. I turned off the buffet lamp and dimmed the chandelier. Someone kept turning it back up, but I was persistent, and the meal and the guests looked wonderful — once the lighting was perfect.

room — at the piano or next to a sofa that isn't up against a wall — without running cords under or over the rug, which is ugly and dangerous.

Dining Rooms

Lighting the dining table should be your main consideration. It will make both the food and the guests look good if the lighting is just right. The size of the chandelier depends on the size of your table, but allow at least 6 inches of clearance on each side of the table so that guests will not bump their heads. Illumination above the

Bedrooms

I like a light switch I can flip on when I walk into the bedroom. For me it doesn't matter if it's for an overhead fixture or bedside lamps (because my bed is near the entrance). Bedside swing-arm reading lamps with three-way bulbs can prevent a lot of bickering between couples. They are a small price for keeping both parties happy.

Hallways

I say, make 'em pretty. Because the ceiling and walls are the only places to decorate, the ceiling is the ideal spot for a pretty light fixture. Hanging lanterns or milk-glass pendants will provide good illumination while looking decorative. Shades with closed bottoms will eliminate harshness from glare.

My house never looks prettier than when it's lighted at night. It is cozy, intimate, warm, welcoming, friendly, engaging, functional, and literate. How can I tell it's literate? By the properly positioned, shaded, and outfitted-with-the-right-bulb-and-wattage reading lamps that are visible everywhere.

LIGHTING FIXTURES

Choosing among all the available lighting options isn't easy. Scale is always more important than style. The chandelier does not have to match the sconces or even be of the same style or era. Rather, it must be the right scale, size, and proportion for the dining table and for the room. If it's undersized, hang it low. If it's oversized, hang it high.

My dining room has one six-arm chandelier, a pair of three-arm wall sconces, two lighted china cabinets, a picture light over Uncle Oscar, and a pair of lamps. The room is most inviting and looks best when all of the light sources are illuminated, yet dimmed to an intimate level. I bought the chandelier in Brussels and carried it back on the plane. The sconces are from a flea market in the south of France, and the lamps are from a local antique store. I love them all.

Always combine several types of sources in a room. Antique stores, junk shops, thrift shops, and tag sales are

all wonderful sources for interesting fixtures. Any light fixture, no matter how dingy or dark, can be refinished or rewired. Remember, too, that other objects can be made into lamps. I've seen the bronzed baby shoe, fire nozzle (from a retired fireman), urn, vase, an old newel post, and even a stack of books transformed into a lamp.

Place lamps on both sides of a shared bed.

I say it's not so much what you have but what you do with it that makes any interior work. It's in the mix. Numerous kinds of light fixtures are on the market. Here are some of the basics styles. Mix them up.

An unusual pendant creates a focal point in this dining room.

Pendants

A pendant hangs down from the ceiling like a pendant from your neck. It comes in many shapes and forms and can be used in many rooms. Pendants can be closed at the bottom, directing light upward, or open at the bottom, directing light downward. If they direct light down and the bulb is above eye level, use a frosted bulb to diminish glare.

Chandeliers

A chandelier is a type of pendant, only more so. It is multi-armed with branches that extend in many directions to disperse light evenly, and not just down onto the table but outward and up toward the ceiling, too. The more arms a chandelier has, the more light.

Because I'm a decorator, I get this question almost every time a customer installs a pendant, chandelier, or hanging fixture of any kind over a table, "How high should it be?" I asked about 12 well-respected lighting dealers, and the answer was universal. There should be 30 to 34 inches between the bottom of the fixture and the top of the table. That's their rule of thumb.

If your chandelier or pendant looks skimpy over your table, hang it on the low side of the dealers' formula (30 inches

GREENHOUSE GLOW

My friend Fran says plants won't live in her house. I know the problem because my charming porch blocks off natural light to some areas of my house. To overcome this, I use lamps as grow lights. I keep the one over my ivy topiaries on 10 hours a day. Sure, I burn a lot of electricity and change bulbs often, but my plants grow and curl up toward the light. This won't work for plants that need direct sun, but plants that thrive in medium light will do very well.

Hang chandeliers where it is easy to reach them when you have to change bulbs.

above the table), or it will appear even smaller than it is. If it looks large, hang it at the high end (34 inches), or it will appear overpowering.

Accessibility. When hanging a chandelier in hard-to-reach places, such as a stairwell or on a cathedral ceiling, changing the bulbs won't be easy. Marcia, a client, has to use a tall stepladder to change the light bulbs in the chandelier in her cathedral-ceilinged master bath. I warned her against the cathedral ceiling for this reason. But once she had it, she needed a chandelier because nothing else was the right scale. This choice was dangerous from the outset with slippery marble floors and no soft landing. Marcia threw her back out moving the tall ladder last week.

Don't be afraid of multiple arms as long as the chandelier is easily accessible. If you put a chandelier with a million arms in a hard-to-reach place, you will mount that tall ladder a million times a year because bulbs never all burn out the same day. Long-lasting bulbs can last twice as long as standard bulbs, but they do not come in every size and shape. If you require candelabra-type bulbs, you're out of luck. They only come as strong as 60 watts. There are flame-tip or torpedo-tip ones. If you are thinking of dressing the bulbs up with lampshades, use torpedo-tip bulbs.

Another way to dress up a chandelier is with a *bobeche*. This is the little collar or plate at the base of a chandelier. It can also be used with a candlestick lamp. Originally designed to catch wax drippings, a bobeche continues now as ornament or on chandelier-type fixtures.

Sconces

A sconce is a wall-mounted light fixture. Generally, sconces should be installed about 60 to 70 inches up from the floor, depending on the ceiling height. In the case of a sconce with a curved arm, such as the type that simulates a candleholder, the direction of the arm will help you figure out exactly where to put the electrical socket. If the sconce curves up, hang it at the lower, 60-inch range and at the higher range if it curves down.

When a sconce faces toward the ceiling, it illuminates much more universally than when it faces down. Try it with

A small shade cuts the glare from this sconce's bulb.

a twist-arm lamp if you don't believe me. Virtually all bathroom sconces should face down. Otherwise heat and moisture will get trapped inside the shade. As a result, the bulb and even the fixture will burn out frequently.

Mantel sconces. On two recent jobs, I found sconces that were positioned too low over the mantels. They looked crowded, as if they were sitting there. When the electricians located the wiring, they must have based the position of the socket on the height of the fireplace opening or surround, without factoring in the height of the mantel. Sconces should sit at least 10 inches above the mantel, but 14 to 16 inches is usually better.

Lamps

In this book, when I refer to lamps, I am talking about the flexible, portable sources of light in a room that can be added or subtracted without an electrician. You just plug them into an existing outlet. The placement of lamps is very important. If you're going to read, write, or work by lamplight, you shouldn't be in your own shadow. Lamps provide localized pools of light, charming and cozy as long as there is no glare. To prevent glare, the bottom of the shade should be at eye level when you're seated so you're not looking up into the bulb. But this rule doesn't work when I nap on my sectional. Looking up at a lightbulb drives me crazy. In this case, a lamp with a covered bulb, like those old-fashioned ones with an interior milk-glass bowl and an outer shade, or a converted oil lamp with a globe, would prevent the problem.

Torchères

This is another type of floor lamp. It is usually a tall, thin, standing lamp that directs light toward the ceiling. Against a light or white ceiling, it can bounce off a good deal of illumination. It's not a good idea to try this with a ceiling that has been painted a color. If you read the chapter on color, you'd know that colored ceilings are almost never recommended.

Halogen bulbs are often used with torchieres because the ceiling does not object to glare, so these bulbs can generate their bright, white light without offense. As furnishings, torchères are dramatic, too, and great for adding light in corners where you don't have room for a table lamp.

This uplight is dramatic but provides little illumination.

Track Lights

Track lights can be used for general lighting or for spot-lighting. The heads of these fixtures are clipped onto a ceiling-mounted track. Their advantage is flexibility. Lights can be added or subtracted and angled to high-light art or a specific area. Sometimes, you can switch the housing for another style, but basically you don't have a lot of variety from which to choose.

A disadvantage is the metal track across the ceiling, which is usually unattractive. Because the lights are set at an angle, exposing the bulb, track lights inevitably shine into someone's eyes, and the person has to avoid glare. I am always twisting and turning them to find the right, glare-free pitch. Track lighting goes in and out of style. Look for unobtrusive miniature versions.

Track lights are adjustable. Use them to highlight art or as spotlights.

Small recessed lights enhance this showcase for books and art.

Ceiling-Mounted Fixtures

While ceiling-mounted fixtures come from the same electrical box as a pendant, they do not hang down. They sit on the ceiling the way a stud earring sits on the ear. Surface-mounted ceiling fixtures will illuminate a large area, so they are used for general light.

Recessed Lights

Their look is architectural, and their light dispersion is confined and limited. You need an awful lot of recessed lights to get the amount of illumination achieved with a single ceiling-mounted fixture. I have three in my kitchen over the work surface by the sink. They work fine. But if you need a lot of them, the ceiling will look spotty, all punctured and pockmarked. When planning recessed lighting, be sure to lay out a nice even grid that will form a neat, uniform pattern on the ceiling. You can arrange recessed fixtures in a straight line, in a square, or in a circular pattern, for example. Avoid a random pattern, which can look cluttered, and always try to use just enough recessed lights to provide the maximum amount of light you need.

Canister Lights. To eliminate glare, install the kind of recessed fixtures that place the bulb high inside the canister. No one likes to stare at a naked lightbulb. It's hard on the eye, and it makes all tasks, from reading to slicing, difficult. Once upon a time, recessed ceiling lights beamed directly and unflatteringly straight down. Now you can direct *eyeball* fixtures to accent art or illuminate a particular work area. These can even be angled to distribute light in a general manner.

Hi hats, or recessed canister lights, get their name from their shape, which is like a high top hat or a coffee can. Only their metal rims are exposed. Before even considering hi hats, make sure the area above your ceiling is high enough to accommodate them. Hi hats don't illuminate a room as much as they create beams of light that, like a headlight or a flashlight, start narrow and widen into a conical ray. Think about a spotlight on your head. It's not attractive, nor is it comfortable. Mounted close to the wall, hi hats can create a disturbing scalloped effect. That doesn't mean you shouldn't use these fixtures. Just don't install them directly above where people will be standing

LAMPLIGHT IN THE WINDOW

Don't ask me why, but every good architect I have worked with specifies a recessed light about 24 inches from all the windows or French doors on the ground floor. This is not for function because these close-to-the-wall spots are rarely used. It's for atmosphere at night. If you can't do this, a lamp on a chest in front of the window can look just as welcoming.

Work with your electrician to create a plan for recessed fixtures.

or sitting. They are great in corners, in front of windows, and around nooks and crannies. I don't recommend them for task lighting, however. Take the kitchen of one of my earliest clients, Muriel. The ceiling was littered with these fixtures and yet when Muriel leaned over to slice a tomato, she was working in her own shadow.

Too often people add hi hats with abandon, leaving the ceiling looking like Swiss cheese. Design your ceiling-light layout with care and precision. And don't overdo it. With new code requirements, such as one in Scarsdale that calls for sprinkler systems, and technology, such as alarm systems and audio speakers, ceilings are beginning to look like littered parking lots after a parade. Keep it clean. We want to look at the room, not the ceiling or the lights.

WORKING WITH ELECTRICIANS

Chandeliers, table lamps, recessed lights—all types of lighting are powered from the same electrical source. Your electrician will need to run wires and install boxes, giving you time to select the appropriate fixtures. The first decision you must make is how many connections and outlets you want and where to put them. Don't expect the electrician to tell you how high to hang the chandelier or to recommend the type of dimmer switch to use, either. Although you're not the expert, you'll probably have to make these decisions.

It has been my experience that it's important to make sure your electrican folds a little extra wire into the fixture box in case you have to make an adjustment. Maybe you're not exactly sure where a ceiling fixture will be located. Or you may want a pendant over a kitchen island that has both a sink and an overhang for seating. You may not know early on if you need more headroom near the sink and less by the seating area. That additional wire will give you some leeway to move the fixture.

Divide and Conquer

If you want to control the lighting in both the upstairs and downstairs hallways or both indoor and outdoor lights all from the top of your stairs, put them on separate switches. Mount one switch for the upstairs hall lights above another one for the down-stairs hall lights to eliminate confusion. Makes sense, doesn't it?

For this installation, the reading lights and the uplights are on separate controls.

CHAPTER 7

THE TV ROOM

At my house, there has been only one gift that all of us, even guests and friends, have liked and benefited from equally: **a big-screen TV**. We put one under our Christmas tree five years ago, and it is truly the gift that has kept on giving. Whether we want to admit it or not, the **television is the hearth** of the **twenty-first century**. It is our version of a town square, the information center where we find out **what's happening in the world**, what the weather will be tomorrow, or who won the game last night. The TV will only **gain more prominence** in our households as it becomes an **interactive computer** as well. So instead of trying to pretend the TV doesn't exist and that we don't really **watch it an average of 21 hours** a week, according to some sources, why don't we learn how to make it **part of our homes**?

Once families gathered in front of the fire. Today we're getting together to watch TV or a movie. That's why it makes sense to design a TV room that accommodates our comfort needs as well as the equipment.

A kitchen TV fits nicely on a cabinet shelf.

TV VIEWING BY DESIGN

Something we had to address once we acquired our behemoth TV set was, where should it go? At first we put it on an antique trunk where its smaller predecessor had resided. But the new TV boasted a 40-inch screen, whereas our old one had been a "little bitty" 21-incher. Our big-screen TV (defined as anything 40 inches or larger) was indeed tipsy and wobbly sitting atop the trunk. So we decided to welcome this new addition to our household by giving it a proper home.

The best thing we did was to build a corner cabinet that raised the TV 42 inches off the floor. This positioned the screen high enough above our seated heads to allow

unobstructed viewing and a lot less infighting. Previously, my viewing was either to the right or left of my husband's propped-up feet. Seating for our family of six (not to mention visitors) necessitated an L-shape arrangement in the form of either a sectional or two sofas. I prefer a sectional because you lose two arms and gain another seat. And because we placed the TV on the diagonal, there is equal viewing access from both wings of the sectional.

More Ideas. Where else can you put the TV? Anywhere you want to watch it. I have put a television over the refrigerator, under a kitchen wall cabinet, in a hydraulic bench, at the foot of the bed and, of course, in the old reliable armoire. It's noteworthy that the sales of home-entertainment units have driven the growth of the furniture industry in recent years. But wherever you decide to place the TV, a few guidelines will make your viewing hours comfortable, safe, and pleasurable — and will help the TV room stand up to regular, rugged use in style.

Get Real: Furnishings

The TV room probably gets the most use of any room in the house. Children play here, dogs nap, and we all snack in front of the TV. Like the kitchen in our house, and unlike the living or dining rooms, the TV room never gets a day off. This is not the place for delicate and fragile furnishings. Fabrics and surfaces have

We raised our TV 42 inches off the floor for comfortable family viewing.

The sectional sofa in our TV room accommodates our family of six. Its durable fabric holds up to everyday use.

to be sturdy, solid, and washable. Seating should be soft and welcoming, not stiff and upright. The coffee table should be high enough to eat from, low and comfortable enough to prop up your legs, and tough enough to withstand an impromptu dance performance in front of Barney. Don't delude yourself: food will be dropped; beverages will spill. Durable woven yarn-dyed fabrics (versus cotton prints) are best here, as are patterned, low-pile carpets. Solid carpets show stains and spills, and deep-pile carpets become the recipients of scraps and crumbs. Try one of the new generation of Berbers, sisals, or industrials (low-pile looped carpets with a subtle mix of colors and textures).

Tough Enough. Country furnishings with worn finishes only become more attractive with the "imprint" of your own family etched into their grain. No veneers, glass, lacquers, or high shines in this domain. Rather, choose solid-wood surfaces that can be sanded down and refinished when they become too marred and coated with the detritus of daily life. I recently discovered that the entire side of my pine coffee table had been worn down over the years by my children. So we hand-sanded and waxed the table with little effort and great results.

Color It Warm. White rooms reflect light, especially in daylight. (Think beach; think glare.) Rooms designed for TV viewing should be decorated

"Durable woven yarn-dyed fabrics are best here, as are patterned, low-pile carpets."

in warm tones such as deep neutrals like Mocha or Cappuccino all the way to cozy darks. So, remember: dark colors absorb light. White and light colors reflect it.

Lighting. If you're going to be viewing, you might as well do it right. A good rule of thumb is that no light should be brighter than the TV screen. Instead of one bright light source, use several low-level lights. Three-way bulbs or dimmers are often the best solution. Either way, you can set lights low for viewing, and then adjust them higher for reading. Preferably, all light sources should be behind you and not between you and the screen, which can cause eye fatigue.

A flat-screen TV looks like a picture on a wall.

Plump upholstered seating and carpeting combat sound distractions.

Lamps can also cause glare and distracting reflections on the screen, so use black or dark lampshades rather than white or light-color ones to eliminate the problem. Also, don't position the television directly across from a window, which can invite sun glare. Shutters or wooden blinds are the best way to control and direct incoming light (up toward the ceiling or down to the floor), so you can comfortably watch TV during the day.

Materials and Surfaces. Avoid too many hard, sound-reflective surfaces, or you'll have what is technically known as "picture-sound distortion." That's when the picture is directly in front of you, but the sound is bouncing all over the room. In my house, when there's a car chase on the screen, it sounds like it's happening just outside the front door. Skylights, tile floors, stone, marble, and glass all add up to sound distortion. Think movie-theater comfort instead: rugs, upholstery, curtains. Soft surfaces absorb sound.

Keep It Simple. This is not the room for overblown floral wallpaper or masses of knickknacks surrounding the television. Clutter makes it more difficult to focus on the picture. Create a muted solid or small-patterned back-

"Like everything in technology land, prices continually decline while quality goes up."

ground instead. Move videotapes, the stereo, CDs, and other electronic gear to another wall, or hide them behind cabinet doors. Who says every video you've ever watched has to be located next to the TV? Consider storing tapes and disks elsewhere, in a closet, trunk, or basket.

FAST FORWARD

Television is over 50 years old. Like everything in technology land, prices continually decline while quality goes up. In the 1960s, TVs were built into consoles. We paid more for the cabinet than the electronics. Then along came "video" in the 1970s. Remember what VCRs first cost? By the 1980s, renting a movie became a Saturday night ritual in many households.

Now we are in an era when the technological and electronic rate of change is accelerating. It seems that every day there is some new technology that we must have. For those of us who are still stuck in the console era, here are some terms that are becoming part of twenty-first-century TV vernacular.

High-Definition TV. Also called HDTV, it brings home double the clarity of today's standard television. HDTV has 1125 lines of resolution as opposed to the 525 lines that we watch now on standard TVs—no matter what the size of your screen. With HDTV you get a superlative picture—it's almost as if you're looking out a window. Having just visited friends with HDTV, I can vouch for the superiority of this technology.

Direct View. This is generally what you and I think of as regular old TV,

Soft lighting that can be easily adjusted down is conducive to big-screen viewing.

TUBE TALK

▶ I once read that there are 52 TV sets sold every minute, 24 hours a day, 365 days a year in the United States.

▶ Did you know that Americans spend one-third of all leisure time watching television — four times more than any other leisure activity.

▶ According to the American Academy of Pediatrics, the average American child or adolescent spends more than 21 hours a week watching television, and that isn't even including time spent watching movies and playing video and computer games. The good news is that children are watching one hour less a day than they were five years ago, but guess why? The Internet has supplanted some viewing.

▶ Like all things in technoland, prices have declined since television first appeared on the market. In 1946, a 10-inch black-and-white set sold for about $3,400 in today's money. My advice is: wait a couple of years before buying new technology; the prices will inevitably drop.

▶ What is HDTV? Your current set has 525 lines of resolution; HDTV, or high-definition TV, boasts 1125 lines of resolution, so you get a superlative picture — almost like looking out a window.

as opposed to rear- or front-projection TV. What are its limitations? The maximum screen size is 36 to 38 inches and the monitor is deep, 23 to 25 inches, and bulky. Advantages? It is still one of the best-quality pictures available, and the cost is relatively low. Today you can buy a 19-inch color TV for less than $200. Direct-view TVs are also easy to install. Just plug them in, and attach the cable wire. And unlike some other types of TVs, they can be viewed in ambient light. (In lighting language, that's with the room lights on.)

A small TV in a little quiet corner is perfect for watching the news.

Rear Projection. This is big-screen TV. Now that I've got one, I realize that the picture's not that good. But then again, we sit so far away from it because of the screen's size that it doesn't matter much. Still, I wish I had a better picture. The advantages include the same ease of installation as direct-view TV. And a rear-projection TV is self-contained. It's essentially a big box hooked up to a couple of wires. The biggest plus is the screen size, which is almost unlimited — 40 to 80 inches — but the picture is inferior. If I had known, I probably would have compromised and purchased a 36-inch direct-view TV over my 40-inch rear-projection model. Other drawbacks are a bulky size and a somewhat limited viewing angle. Translation: it's best viewed at eye-level and straight-on. That's not great for kids who are on the floor looking up or for anyone who is on either side. As with direct-view TV, you can also watch rear-projection TV with the lights on.

"You should have the option to add more features, and bells and whistles, down the road of life."

Front Projection. This is a TV system that consists of a separate screen, which can either drop down from the ceiling or is fixed on the wall, plus a projector that is mounted at ceiling height across the room from the screen. It's something like a movie-theater system. Front projection is *very* expensive, and you will need a professional to install it. Front projection is also very light-sensitive. A lighted lamp in the room can wash out whatever is on the screen. Why even consider it, you might ask? I was always skeptical about front projection but not anymore. The picture is *great*. Having just vacationed in a home with front-projection TV, and as a movie lover, I was suitably impressed. Parchment-shaded lamps, as opposed to white ones that reflect the light, allowed me to keep the lights on low in the room while I watched TV—and sorted my mail and read magazines. The projector was couched in the same parchment material as the lampshades, so it was fairly inconspicuous. The screen rose and fell at the press of a button. The entire family loved it, although we did have some programming issues and a problem shutting off the sound at one point. We'll figure that out next time.

Speakers mounted on either side of the monitor enhance this home's video system.

KEEP YOUR DISTANCE!

The ideal distance for safe TV viewing is about 5 times the diagonal width of the TV screen. A 32-inch screen means you should ideally be sitting about 13 feet from the screen. Sure, most children tend to curl up on the floor much closer than this, but sitting too close to the screen might cause eyestrain.

ALL WIRED UP— ENTERTAINMENT SYSTEMS

The most common mistakes people make when planning an audio-video system for a new home are simply oversights. People overlook all low-voltage, stereo communications, cable TV, and satellite wiring and hookups until the last minute. The concept of "systems integration" is new to us. We don't always know what we want until we are exposed to it, and often that's too late in the process, after the walls have been closed up, the electrician has left, and the paint has dried. *Before* it's too late, consider: Where do you want to put the system? What size system do you want? From where do you want to control it? I tell clients that it's always best to overwire a house. That doesn't mean you have to have a state-of-the-art system, a terminal, or even a phone yet. You should have the option to add more features, and bells and whistles, down the road of life.

Audio

Sound should be factored into any consideration of home entertainment. This is an area that has evolved enormously in the last 20 years, exactly when I last made a serious audio purchase. Way back then what we called a serious audio system was usually limited to one room and a pair of ungainly 4-foot-high speakers and a tape deck. With the advent of high-quality speakers that have greatly improved in sound but come in much smaller housings, it was time for me to update. So last Christmas, I treated myself to a new system.

Given the amount of money and time we spend on home entertainment, I recommend a consultation with a professional. The speakers in

In this family room, left, the TV and audio equipment is housed behind a custom cabinet. A slide-out tray holds the monitor, below.

our home work together or independently. I used old speakers, as they are fairly small sized, in the living and dining rooms — after all, you can always upgrade the speakers without mess or travail if they are not in-the-wall models. In the kitchen, I installed new in-the-wall speakers. Now my weekends in the kitchen are infinitely more pleasant, and my dance moves are improving. When the music is blaring throughout the first floor, I just blame it on the kids. Hmmm — I should have thought about extending the sound outside. Maybe next summer I'll do that.

Enhanced Viewing

The last essential element is the video cassette recorder (VCR) or digital video disk (DVD) player. Most households own a VCR, and unlike a DVD player, you can record your favorite shows on it. But due to its high-quality digital output, a DVD offers a greatly enhanced picture. Because one DVD can store so much information, it can usually contain multiple versions of a movie such as standard and letterbox form, as well as different language soundtracks and subtitles. The lesson? Own both if you can.

Custom Cabinets

According to the U.S. Fire Administration, more than two million fires occur each year, and one cause for this can be overheated electronics. Typically we build our stereo and TV into close-fitting cabinets. We turn off the TV or stereo receiver but forget about the VCR or CD player, close the cabinet, and go on vacation. The result can be returning home to a pile of burned rubble. Built-in electronics need air around them for ventilation.

Designing or building an entertainment unit is far less complicated than most people imagine. Almost all components except the TV set are about the same size, so

HOME THEATER

Today many homeowners are considering incorporating a home theater into their homes. According to the Consumer Electronics Association, all you need to equip your home theater is a 25-inch (or larger) TV, a hi-fi/stereo VCR or DVD (Digital Video Disc) player (or both), a surround-sound stereo receiver, and five speakers.

A "you are there" experience can be created in the home with the speakers. The left and right units work similarly to the ones you have hooked up to your stereo. If you space them far apart, you will get a richer sound experience. Keep moving them until you get the desired effect, perhaps on each end of the seating area. The center speaker is for the dialogue, so the actors are not drowned out by the background sound. Finally, the last two speakers add the full movie-theater surround-sound.

you can just build a rack system that consists of a series of uniform slots, approximately 7 inches high x 18 inches wide x 18 inches deep. This should be sufficient to hold the VCR, tape deck, CD player, DVD player, and amplifier. But just to be sure, always measure each component separately. Only the turntable (if you still have one) and the TV will require more room. Position electronic components at eye level (or at least in a range between the top of your head and your hips) for easy operating. Use the topmost and lowest shelves for decorative or lesser-used items.

With the advent of HDTV, digital cable, flat screens, and increasingly sophisticated home theaters, it's clear that TV viewing will only increase. So why not create a room that is truly designed for comfortable viewing?

The front-projection screen drops down for viewing.

CHAPTER 8

HOME OFFICE

Working at home is not a new phenomenon. Until the **industrial revolution** and the factories of the nineteenth century, home was the **workplace** for most people. Then the **transportation revolution** of the twentieth century made it possible for us to commute long distances daily across highways to jobs in other cities and towns. Ironically, the technology of the **twenty-first century** is driving us back again. Today we're trading the corner office for the home office, which may be located in its own separate room or in **any nook or cranny** we can spare. In any case, thanks to the home computer, the office or study is becoming the **hub of the household** in our information-driven world. In this chapter, I'll discuss how to create a **comfortable, attractive, and efficient** work space in your home. You'll also find tips for incorporating the **computer** into your life.

The home computer is an important element in most American households.

FROM THE PROFESSIONALS

People who design computer systems offer this advice for using your home computer:

▶ Purchase a 17-inch or larger monitor. This will let you use larger icons and text sizes, as well as larger images.

▶ Always sit at least 17 inches from the monitor. Give your eyes a break every 15 minutes. Roll your eyes up, down, right, and left to reduce eyestrain, which can cause headaches.

▶ Keep the angle of your wrists slightly higher than the keyboard.

▶ Use a mouse pad with a nonskid surface. This will provide the right amount of friction to give your mouse accurate movement.

▶ Install a surge protector that will protect your modem as well. Check the warranty. Beware of cheaper types (less than $25). If you have frequent power outages, buy an Uninterruptible Power Supply (UPS), which will give you 5 to 15 minutes of system use (to properly save and shut down) if there is an outage.

▶ Don't rely on "brand-name" computers. Most computers have the same manufacturer's hardware and software. The difference is in the operating systems. (Windows and Mac OS are operating systems, for example.)

I know I would benefit from better organization in my home office. Every year when I address the invitations to our annual Christmas party, I wonder why I don't have a computer file with this information. It would make life easier if I didn't have to dredge up multiple lists of names and addresses, some current and some not. Organizing an up-to-date list on my computer is something I will do this year! In fact, the computer is becoming such an integral part of my life that, when mine caught its first virus recently, I felt like a bird that had fallen out of the nest with no home and no place to light—lost, displaced, and discombobulated.

LIVING WITH TECHNO-CREEP

Some experts believe that telecommuting is growing at a clip of 20 percent or more a year. In 1993 only 90,000 individuals were on-line, mostly academics or business people. By 2000 that number has increased by millions. If you haven't created your own Web site by now, what are you waiting for? And in the meantime, have you set aside a planned space in your home to do your telecommuting?

Friends tell me that soon every room in the house will be wired, everyone will have a laptop, and the computer room will become an anachronism. Yeah, sure, like the TV room. We have TVs in lots of places in my house, but a room is still set aside for dedicated

Adjustable shades are required here to control glare.

This home study provides a quiet place for reading.

TV and movie viewing, just as there will always be a home office — even with our laptops to go and the computers in the kids' rooms. The study is where we keep the main computer, the one with all the bells and whistles and the big-screen monitor, plus all of the amenities: a color printer, speakers, a scanner, and a CD burner. It's a very popular spot in our house.

The Computer Room: Only One?

Today's home office isn't reserved for one family member or for one function, either. It isn't just for doing homework or business reports, class lists or car-pooling schedules. It holds its own against the kitchen and TV room as "family central," a place where everyone gravitates, sometimes at once. As a result, I have increasingly more requests to design his-and-her home offices. My friend Michelle's husband, an academic and a writer, finds it difficult to work while others are in "his" office. So Michelle and Frank are now talking renovation to provide a second office for her and the kids. I understand. Just last night I was trying to do a phone interview for this book while my teenage son was on the computer in the same room. Odd sounds ebbed and flowed from some strange Web site. My son and I exchanged impatient looks until finally I signaled "go away" in sotto voce.

"If you haven't created your own Web site by now, what are you waiting for?"

Location, Location

As with any hub, the home office is an anchor, so it should be conveniently located, not tucked away in a cabinet or buried under the stairs. Yet some homeowners stick their computers or workstations anywhere in the basement, the attic, or even in a closet. Talk about stagnant air! What are they trying to hide? A computer is not a family skeleton, it is a sign of intelligent life. Instead of relegating the computer to the basement, put it in a practical location with little traffic and less noise. Hang a bulletin board on the wall. Add some lighting, a place for filing paperwork, shelves for reference manuals, phone books, and school directories.

Choose Convenience. Set up your home office where you want to be and where you want your kids to be. It can be a room set aside for a dedicated office, or you could create an integrated office, which essentially means your desk may be in the kitchen. I like to be near the front door. After all, the real winners of e-commerce are the delivery services. How can I order things via the Internet and not be next to the door when UPS arrives? Or check a pot on the stove? Or get a soft drink? Our house came with a small study between the kitchen and the entrance hall. How lucky can we be? We would have been luckier if only we had two of them, one for the kids and one for the adults. Above all, locate your home office where you're likely to use it: where it is accessible and can accommodate your need to do several tasks, sometimes, at once.

Places to Consider

Theoretically, if you are meeting the demands of the IRS, the home office can go anywhere. Even if you're not earning income, you're still managing a household. If you're like me, that means paying bills, organizing paperwork, and handling all the details of family life. This is complicated work, and it warrants a well-planned area.

Shared Spaces. For those without the luxury of a spare room, part of a bedroom is often the most common option in many homes. You might have the monitor, hard drive, printer, TV, and underwear drawer next to one another. This is great unless it's *your* bedroom and there's a cavalcade of kids trooping in to use the computer. Instead, I suggest locating the work space where it isn't a disruption. Consider the living room. Why not? Correct lighting and the right arrangement of furniture can create the illusion of a separate space.

In fact, the computer and a small workstation can be integrated into other underused rooms. The dining room and the guest room are two likely candidates.

Found Room. I also suggest using "dead space" or an underutilized area. Wherever you put it, don't place the computer over the heat or air-return. They blow too much dust, although I wonder if we keep the same equipment long enough for it to get dirty, let alone age. This includes hallways, corners, or areas under the stairs.

Kids and computers are a natural pair, but you may want to supervise time on-line.

Kids and Computers

Teenagers spend more time using the Internet than do adults. They use it as a tool for school, for talking on-line with friends, for exploring, and for playing games. When teens meet in person, they often ask for e-mail addresses instead of phone numbers. For the first time since TV entered our lives, it has competition. I read a report that estimated as much as 25 percent of prime-time viewing has been replaced with Internet surfing.

If you have children, you'll want them to use the computer in an open environment so that you'll know what they're doing. If you don't put a TV in the kids' room, don't put a computer there either. This advice comes from a childless computer expert, not just from me—a busybody mother. At our house, we put our old computers in the kids' rooms, but Internet surfing is only

"If you don't put a TV in the kids' room, don't put a computer there either."

A large computer armoire can also house a fax, files, and supplies.

possible from the main computer in the study. That way we know what the kids are up to. Besides, for us, a bedroom is a retreat at the end of the day, not a place to isolate ourselves, which can happen when too much time is spent on the computer.

Out in the Open
Or Behind Closed Doors?

If you have limited space, decide whether you want your office equipment out in the open or behind doors, now called, respectively, a visible work environment (VWE) or a subtle work environment (SWE). When I read articles on home computers, they always say, "If you put it in an armoire, you can close the doors and it's gone." Well, if you insist on "behind closed doors," you may need a computer armoire. But there are problems beyond just poor air circulation. Certainly the sales for this kind of furniture support its popularity, but the technical requirements of the equipment and the physical volume of the computer components make these pieces big and bulky. However, some are more attractive than others.

Armoire Doors. Another problem arises with computer armoires because the doors are left open most of the time. So, instead of receiving proper support from the frame, the doors are braced by the hinges, which will begin to sag under the weight. Leveling the cabinet doors and

" . . . while technology is getting bigger, the tools of technology are becoming smaller. "

adjusting and replacing hinges becomes a common repair job. But don't forget that while technology is getting bigger, the tools of technology are becoming smaller. You don't need a huge monitor. Besides, electronics are chic today. Why not leave them in view?

You may base your decision on how often you will use the area. Certainly if you have limited space, and the home

A closet isn't the ideal "office," but if you must, light it well and ventilate it.

A neat work area, left, improves efficiency. Built-in housings for components, below, keep the desktop clear.

office is in the living room, you'll have to make some concessions. In my clients Marjorie and Peter's compact city apartment, we did not hide the computer behind closed doors. Rather, we put it in an open unit on a wall that is not visible as you enter the room or even when the room is inhabited for other purposes, for the most part. From its most commonly seen side, the unit looks like a handsome piece of cabinetry. We had it built into the room, but designed it to be removable in case the couple uproots to a larger home in the suburbs.

Lifestyles Matter

Sometimes customers with small children don't understand the impact that the computer will have on their kids, nor do they know what to do about it. One former client, with children ages three and five, wanted to put the computer in the laundry room. Computers and home offices are not just about work, although that is certainly a part of it. For the pre-adolescent, the computer is socialization, exploration, and information. For the younger child the computer is games, language, learning skills, and visuals. In our house, the desk went from a single, albeit large, surface that held a solitary computer to an L-shaped, carpenter-built, family-designed worktable and storage unit. We kept the large, "picnic-table" surface and added a carpenter-built

Some home offices can be part of a larger multi-purpose room.

In an architect's home office, there's room for flat files, left, and a drawing table, below.

return unit with drawers, storage, and more surface. No matter how much of a neatnik you are, it is virtually impossible to keep all the little bits—stamps (are they an anachronism yet?), paper clips, staples, pencils, pens, erasers, labels, notepads, envelopes—in place. A divided drawer goes a long way toward keeping a desk surface clear. Our two pieces, the "picnic table" and the desk-height storage piece, accommodate two computers, speakers, CD burners, a couple of color printers, and every shape and form of youthful detritus. The computer table once sat relatively close to one side of the room, perpendicular to the window; now it is in the center of the room commanding its rightful place in our home. Where once there was a single chair, now there are two chairs—on each side of the table. Still with all this, we have arguments over whose turn it is to sit down at the computer . . . and it's usually never mine.

FUNCTION FIRST

Home offices should be designed around their components—equipment, furniture, work surfaces, lighting, and the people who will use these spaces. Once you establish where to put the computer, think about the tasks you'll be doing. Word processing? Faxing? Typing up class lists? E-mailing your grandchildren? E-mailing your grandparents? Is the space just for you or is it shared with the kids or your spouse? Your answers will help you assess what you'll need. Don't forget to include an addi-

tional phone line (or two) and enough electrical outlets. When space is limited, people are inclined to put two or more computers in the same room, often on the same work surface. If this is your situation, you'll have to create boundaries. They define territory—yours, mine, and ours.

Defining Personal Space. File drawers or a printer or scanner cabinet can act as a divider to separate your place on the work surface from your partner's. If the cabinet protrudes above the desktop, it will keep paper and minutiae from spilling from one person's work area into another's.

If kids share your office, a desk surface that's long enough for two children to sit side by side is a good idea. An ideal length is about 48 inches. However, it could extend to any length that you can fit into the room's layout, but 42 inches should be the minimum. Design a floor plan that places the adults in the inner zone of the layout and the children on the outer perimeter. That way, kids can run in and out

"Don't forget to include an additional phone line (or two) and enough electrical outlets."

A keyboard tray places the keys and the mouse at a comfortable height.

of the room without disturbing you (hopefully) or leaving their soda cans and candy wrappers on *your* desktop.

Ergonomics: Healthy Comfort

Ergonomics is more than a buzzword, it is the study of how workers function in their environments in general and in respect to their equipment in particular. Nowhere is it more important than in the home office when you are determining how to place the computer screen, the keyboard, and the chair. Regardless of the size or configuration of your home office, you need an ample horizontal surface for the VDU. That's tech talk for the video display unit, more commonly known as the monitor or screen, and the keyboard. If only adults are using the monitor, a surface-area of 24 to 30 inches may be adequate if meager. However, if children will use the computer, they'll need 48 inches or more to spread out because kids will gather in front of the monitor the way they do in front of the TV. Experts also recommend positioning the monitor dead ahead. Otherwise you will have to tilt your head at a stressful angle.

Keyboard comfort. To reduce strain on the hands, arms, and shoulders, ergonomics gurus say the keyboard should be no higher than 29 inches, preferably 27 inches, from the floor. That's nothing new. It used to be called the "secretarial return" before computers. (I like to refer to this era as B.C.) A desktop or tabletop is traditionally 29 inches high. At 27 inches a pullout mechanism lowers the keyboard to the ergonomically recommended height. People often buy desks that come equipped with these pullout trays, but they never use them.

Experts say a five-wheel-base chair offers maximum stability.

You should. You can also buy one from any office-supply source and easily install it under an existing desktop.

The Importance of Good Support

Keyboards are now designed ergonomically with several adjustable arm supports. I can't get used to them, but I don't make my living at a computer, even if I do use it up to 15 hours a week. This may seem trivial, but when we think of how many years our children will spend in front of the monitor, adjustable arm supports take on more importance. I have an acquaintance, a once-prolific writer, who has such severe carpal tunnel syndrome that she can type only for an hour a day now.

Avoiding Injuries. If you're used to working one way, it's difficult to adjust to something else, even if it's better for you. For example, I can't use the continuous pad that goes in front of the keyboard to support the wrists because it feels constricting to me. Bad habits die hard, I guess. However, if you're starting from scratch, why not train yourself the right way and educate your children in the process to avoid painful repetitive stress injuries?

> *"...educate your children to avoid repetitive stress injuries."*

Alan Hedge, professor of Cornell University's Department of Design and Environmental Analysis, advises that to prevent repetitive strain injuries such as "Nintendo thumb," children who play games at the computer should sit so that their shoulders and upper arms are relaxed. Their wrists should be either parallel to or lower than their forearms (not at the sides or elevated), and their heads should be straight when facing the screen.

If a child complains of sore wrists or a stiff neck, limit computer time to three 20-minute sessions per day with breaks of at least 10 minutes between.

BUY THE RIGHT CHAIR

You will spend more hours than you can imagine in your new home office, and 98 percent of that time will be spent in a chair. Good ergonomics is essential. The front of the chair should tip or tilt forward slightly to allow proper legroom. At a minimum, the chair should be curved at the front so as not to cut off circulation. Everyone talks about the need for a backrest with lumbar support, but when I work my back is seldom resting against the chair. I tend to lean forward, toward the desk. Backrests must be for executives — or maybe for anyone with back problems or people who spend a lot of time at the computer. In any case, you do need a chair with a five-wheel base, the so-called "star" configuration. Yes, ones with a four-wheel base are cheaper. You'll find out why — from the floor — because they tend to tip over.

screen or a hood on your computer screen. An ideal lighting scenario is one that combines indirect overhead illumination with table lamps. Dumb luck. I have just that. Indirect means the light is not shining directly down on you and your work surface but is diffused in the room. You shouldn't use exposed, open-bottom light fixtures. The desktop lamp or task lights illuminate the rest of whatever it is you are doing at your computer.

Easy on the Eyes

Eyestrain is blamed on computers, but it is usually the result of glare bouncing off the screen, either from poorly placed light fixtures or from the sun. Attention to proper lighting (and adjustable window treatments) can eliminate glare and prevent eyestrain.

If possible, place the computer perpendicular to the window or locate it at an inside wall rather than in front of a window. If there's no option but the latter, cover the window with curtains or blinds. Ceiling light reflection can be reduced by using an anti-glare

A laptop computer can turn any quiet spot into an office.

Professional Tips. Paul Marcus of Manhattan Cabinetry in New York City advises that if space is limited, try to minimize anything that will sit on the work surface, such as lamps. Lamps take up space that could be better used for equipment or work. Instead, try to incorporate lighting as part of the work-station structure, either in a hutch on top of the surface or on a separate *light bridge*, a horizontal strip of wood with a light built into it that connects two or more upper cabinets. A light bridge is a great way to free up the surface of your desk if you have limited space. Use an adjustable fixture so that you can deflect glare from the screen, and position the lamp to illuminate the task at hand. It's always a smart idea to install a dimmer switch so that you can modify the light level according to your changing needs.

Don't place lighting directly above your head, either, unless you want to bake all day. Halogens are suitable, providing they're low voltage and generate little heat. I prefer halogens if they're built into a light bridge but not for ceiling mounts. If you are in a tight, confined space, use fluorescent bulbs. (See "Lighting," pages 152–177.) Fluorescents are cool and generate no standing heat.

This shared office allows two people to work comfortably at the same time.

OUTFITTING YOUR OFFICE

Computer options are forever changing. At our house, we got used to a desktop monitor with a separate central processing unit (CPU), sometimes called a "tower," which was located on the floor. Now, however, computer manufacturers are combining the monitor with the CPU, incorporating drives for both a CD and a floppy disk into one unit. The bottom line: the CPU is a component to which you want access. When it was only "the brains," you could hide it away. Now, with the advent of flat-screen monitors that are only 8 inches deep, desktops can be much shallower, which helps you fit your computer into a tighter space and gives you more desktop surface for spreading out paperwork.

"Wood. . .adds a warm, cozy feeling in the midst of all the high-tech equipment."

The downside to a flat-screen monitor is that it's a separate component from the preferable desktop CPU. A separate CPU can be stored on the floor, under the desk. Most desks have a 30-inch-wide kneehole area, and not all of that is needed for legroom.

Arranging Space Around Your Needs

If you have 8 linear feet of space that is 22 inches deep, you can design a work space that includes a bookcase and storage. If you don't have this much space, you can arrange two separate areas, one for the computer and one for storage, that are placed parallel to one another or arranged in an L-shape.

Conserving the Work Surface. The printer can be stored on the desktop if there's room. But because you probably use it less often than other items, you may want to put it below the desk in an open or pull-out drawer, such as the one pictured on page 204. If you have a fax machine, try to put that elsewhere, too. These machines are noisy, and they take up a lot of space. Just make sure the fax has a proper home where the papers won't end up all over the floor.

I recommend a wood surface for your desktop. Leather is soft and cozy, but it stains and scratches, and it's hard to clean. Marble, granite, limestone, or any stone is cold on your forearms. Metal is noisy, it scratches, and it can get hot from equipment. It also reflects glare.

Designing the Work Surface

Paul Marcus likes to use a high-pressure laminate for his custom designs because it wears well. If you want the look of wood, he recommends a plastic laminate with a wood-grain look or a laminate insert on top of the surface in the area that is subject to the most abuse. High-pressure laminate was originally designed for industrial purposes in restaurant kitchens and hospitals, where it is still most often used. Laminate surfaces are less expensive than wood and come in a wide range of colors and patterns. They are not easy to repair, so I suggest that if you use a color, choose a pattern with speckles or flecks that will help hide the inevitable damage that may occur on this much-used surface.

Wood may not be as durable as some types of laminate, but it is long lasting and resilient, and it can be refinished or touched up. Most importantly, it adds a warm, cozy feeling in the midst of all the high-tech equipment.

Also, it's wise to soften the edge on the front of the desk or worktop. If you choose a straight edge, be sure it has an eased pencil edge, which means the sharpness has been worn or softened. A waterfall or a bullnose makes an ideal edge. (See the sketches below.) It's more comfortable to lean against a soft edge.

An elegantly appointed desk never looks high-tech.

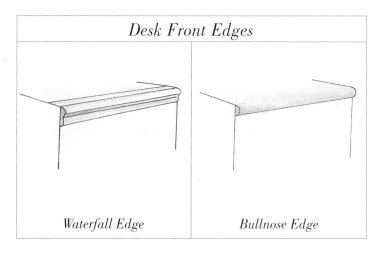

Desk Front Edges

Waterfall Edge   *Bullnose Edge*

The Non-Custom Route

If you're not planning on a custom-built design, you can go to an office supply house or any store that sells office furniture. Some electronics and software manufacturers have joint ventures in retail stores that marry electronics with home furnishings and products that fit into our new techno-centric lifestyle. However, if you want to keep the "home" in home office, I suggest heading to a home furnishings store or shopping at your traditional furniture

haunts (including antiques stores, unfinished furniture shops, flea markets) for at least some of the room's furnishings. My desk is an old trestle table that I bought from under a vendor at the famous Brimfield, Massachusetts, antiques fair. We supplemented this essentially nice-looking "picnic table" with a custom-made piece that houses a printer, copier paper, and several drawers for minutiae such as paper clips and staples. Somehow it is still reassuring that we have low-tech manual hole punchers in our lives.

Wire Management

This is important for safety's sake as well as aesthetics, and it is an important home-office design issue. What with the plethora of accoutrements of home-office electronics, cord-control counts. It's helpful to have computer "grommets," or holes in the desk surface that will carry power cables and wires to wall outlets. But make sure the plugs as well as the wires fit through them. Computer cables often have oval plugs, while standard electrical plugs are more typically round. If you don't measure first or don't have a tryout, you could end up trying to force your cable and computer plugs through a too-tight hole.

Cable organizers and wire holders are commercially available. Hooks installed on the underside of the desk away from where your legs go are another aid in cable management. For a small additional cost, you can have an outlet or phone jack installed on the top of the desk unit itself or mounted on the side of a base cabinet. Your surge protector also can be mounted at the side of or underneath your desk.

Modesty Panels. When the desk is against a wall, be sure that the far side under the work surface is open, so you can access wires. When it's away from a wall, consider a *modesty panel*. This is a vertical panel, perpendicular to the desktop. It can extend to the floor or stop short of it. Initially, modesty panels were designed to provide visual privacy for secretaries at their usually free-floating desks in communal offices. If your desk is deep enough, you can put the modem behind the modesty panel and hide those unsightly wires.

More Organization. Studies indicate that the average American spends five days a year looking for things—the car keys, sunglasses, receipts. In light of that, it's nice to have a small drawer into which to sweep clutter, but a series of boxes and the old coffee mug for pens to sign documents still suffice. I don't have proper file cabinets,

but I keep two metal file boxes in a nearby closed cabinet. I take them out when I need to get access to something.

A locking mechanism for keyboard pullouts will protect them from batters and bumps when not in use. A stationary lock that must be released with a clip before pushing it out of the way is the best option. People are rough when they're working. They are focused on the work and not on maintaining somewhat fragile or vulnerable equipment.

Maintenance Counts!

Use these tips for keeping your home office equipment in good working order.

▶ Don't spray any cleaner on your computer screen unless it is marked specifically for that purpose. Use alcohol pads sold at computer stores or rubbing alcohol on a cotton ball.

▶ Don't spray liquid cleaner on the keyboard. Use a feather duster or a blow dryer on the cool setting. Many experts also use pressurized air in cans, which can be purchased at any computer or office supply store.

▶ Don't let the CPU or tower get dirty. Like refrigerator coils, it needs regular dusting.

CHAPTER 9

KITCHENS

From every standpoint, the importance of the kitchen and its design cannot be underestimated. The heart of the home beats in the kitchen. There's the hum of the refrigerator. The whir of the food processor. The crunch of the garbage disposal. The bubbling of dinner simmering on the stove. These are the reassuring sounds of a home in action. I also see the kitchen as a warehouse, a communications center, a place to socialize, and the hub of family life. According to industry studies, 90 percent of American families eat some or all of their meals in the kitchen. It is also the command center where household bills are paid and vacations are planned. The kitchen is even a playroom at times.

A rich mixture of materials, textures, and colors makes this kitchen friendly and warm. A generous marble-topped island divides the large space into separate zones for cooking, cleanup, and eating.

An undercounter microwave is at a convenient height for the kids.

Emotions, as well as tasks, reside here. This is where you could find mom whenever you needed her. It's where the cookies were kept. When other rooms were cold and empty, the kitchen was a place of warmth and companionship. It is from the kitchen that the family sets off into the day. And it is to the kitchen they return at nightfall.

WHAT DO YOU HAVE IN MIND?

Planning is essential when you're contemplating a new kitchen because so many of its components are "plugged in," so to speak, and not easily relocated. Most

Staples and canned goods are stored in a separate pantry.

of the "furnishings" are installed. Cabinets and appliances are not like sofas you can slide into another room or chairs that can be moved upstairs. In addition to the standard issues of design (light, space, color, window treatments, flooring, seating) are pipes, cables, ducts, vents, waste lines, and appliances—components that support vital functions and are subjected to years of use and abuse. Many tasks can only

be done in the kitchen, and no amount of design should be allowed to interfere with their efficient performance.

Kitchen Value. With its exacting demands of function and family life, the kitchen is perhaps the most complex room of the house to tackle. Certainly, it can also be the most expensive, undoubtedly your most significant investment other than the purchase of a home. Yet, from a financial perspective alone, it is a very worthwhile investment: the National Home Builders Association reports that, dollar-for-dollar, you will get back the investment you make in your kitchen when you sell your home. That's provided you don't install hot pink cabinets. By contrast you get, on average, only a 50 percent return on a family room and just 10 percent for a pool. This is not the place to make a casual mistake.

Get Good Design Help

CKD stands for certified kitchen designer. I thought it was a merger between Calvin Klein and Donna Karan. Wrong! Someone with the initials CKD after his or her name has passed a series of tests and is certified by the National Kitchen and Bath Association (NKBA), an organization of professional kitchen and bath designers and retailers. They are trained in design and remodeling and

are familiar with the latest products and trends. If it is a combined kitchen design/retail firm, you may be locked into purchasing cabinets and other kitchen products from that single source, which will limit your choices. These firms retain both designers and remodelers on their staffs, so you may not need to hire a CKD, but you do need help from someone with a lot of experience designing kitchens specifically. You also need good advice from people who are familiar with kitchens. Talk to a professional chef or caterer, your mom, or your housekeeper. Ask advice from your kitchen cabinet representa-

The kitchen's antique settee provides extra seating for guests who drop by.

Bare windows in this kitchen allow a view of the ocean at the sink.

tive and your countertop installer. A tile expert, too. Gather advice from everyone. Then, equipped with this educated information, follow your instincts.

The job of a kitchen designer—and I certainly count myself in that league—is to help you make the best of your own tastes and preferences; not to reinvent, but to refine your vision. A good designer for any room in the home puts the emphasis on you: your space, your cooking habits, your budget. Plus he or she will teach you tricks of the trade to boot.

Tricks of the Trade. High among mine is the best way to store flatware. (See the illustration, page 245.) This brings to mind how carefully thought out every inch in a kitchen should be. Even one-eighth of an inch can matter, as I discovered. I once ordered an insert with tiny divisions for my silverware drawer to get maximum use of the space. The insert I designed would simply drop into place. I had it made and began filling it. Wow! How incredible! Then I went to drop it into the drawer. You can guess what happened, can't you? I'd failed to allow enough space for the screw behind the drawer's pull knob. Yes, even that fraction of an inch made a difference. Now I know how to make that trick work.

FUNCTION

When I was a design student at Parsons, a noted architecture professor began his class with a discussion on function. Function? I was here to study velvet trimmings and tassels. However, I learned that the most important aspect of kitchen design is making the room work efficiently and with ease. All the rest is decorating. There are a lot of things that make a kitchen a well-engineered masterpiece: the right appliances, ample storage and work surfaces, good lighting and ventilation, to name a few. But all of these things are ancillary to an efficient arrangement of the space.

Layouts That Work

The infamous kitchen triangle: once upon a time it was gospel. It dictated not only where you had to place the stove, the refrigerator, and the sink, but that you keep them equidistant from each other, set at the ends of a triangular shape with a perimeter of no more than 22 linear feet. Personally, these formulas just never work for me. Ever. They don't always address individual habits. (See sample layouts on the next three pages.)

Kitchen triangle advocates are always dealing with an idealized situation that almost never exists. Every space has its quirks and its limitations, unless it is brand new or you have a large budget. Even so, I don't think the formula is correct. It doesn't much matter if my cooktop is

Traffic aisles are an important layout consideration.

Doors and appliance doors should not collide when both are open.

no more than 7 feet from my sink. Over the course of a day, I'm at the sink and the refrigerator constantly, whereas I use the cooktop only a few times. And I don't want to have to walk around an island, stumbling all the way, to get something from the refrigerator, either. A straight-line galley kitchen can work just fine, particularly if there's an island or peninsula to break up the space and divide it into components.

Before designing a layout for your space, ask yourself, for example: How wide of an aisle do I need to allow

Kitchen with Island Cooktop

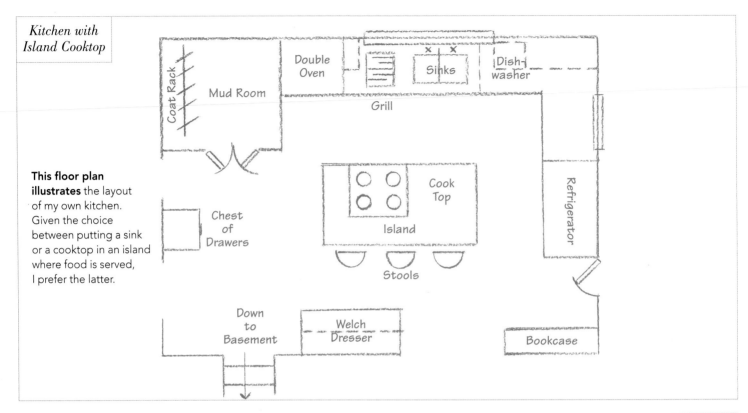

This floor plan illustrates the layout of my own kitchen. Given the choice between putting a sink or a cooktop in an island where food is served, I prefer the latter.

Kitchen with Dining Island

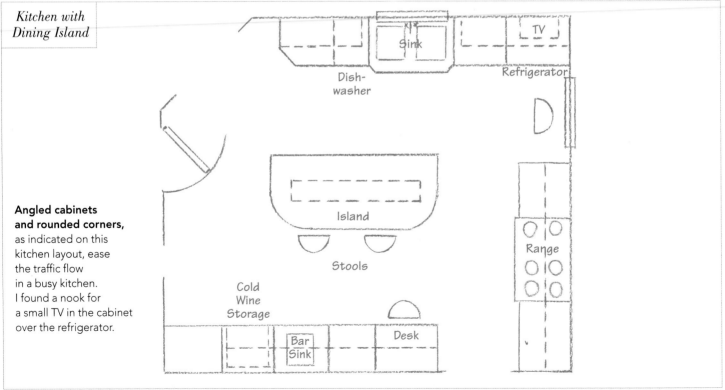

Angled cabinets and rounded corners, as indicated on this kitchen layout, ease the traffic flow in a busy kitchen. I found a nook for a small TV in the cabinet over the refrigerator.

between the sink wall and the island? Or between the refrigerator and the peninsula when the refrigerator door is open? Or between the dishwasher and the sink when I am loading the dishwasher? The answers to these questions are not dictated by rules, but there are guidelines.

Traffic Aisles. At a bare minimum, I allow at least 39 inches between the front of the cabinets and appliances or an opposite-facing island. If it's possible, a clearance of 42 inches is better. And given more available space, a clearance of 48 to 49 inches is lovely. It means that the dishwasher can be open; you can be unloading it, and someone will still be able to walk behind you without doing a side-to-side shuffle or a crab walk. It also means that two people can work together in the same area. Any more than 49 inches, and the space is too much and involves a lot of walking back and forth. Fifty-four inches, for example, is too big a stretch. In large kitchens, there must be balance: make the work areas comfortable, but also keep them compact and efficient so that you don't have to put on roller skates to prepare a small meal.

Food Preparation Areas and Surfaces. In general, I find that much of the food preparation takes place between the sink and the refrigerator. In my old house, that was 24 inches, the width of the top of the dishwasher, and we managed well. In this house, there's 6 feet of space between them. When you think of the work triangle, think of how much and how often you use an appliance. The

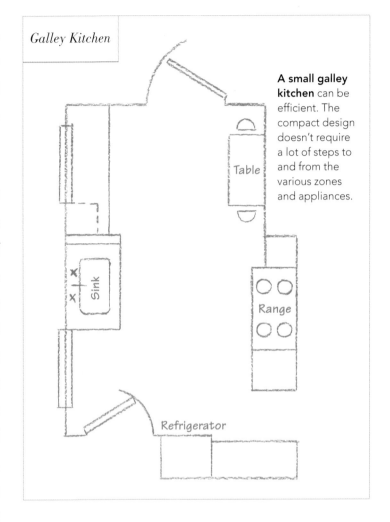

Galley Kitchen

Table

Sink

Range

Refrigerator

A small galley kitchen can be efficient. The compact design doesn't require a lot of steps to and from the various zones and appliances.

sink? Countless times. The refrigerator? Innumerable. The cooktop? Some days, not at all (and certainly not for many breakfasts or lunches today). How close does it really need to be in relation to the sink and refrigerator? Make your primary work zone the link between the sink and the refrigerator; then make the cooktop a secondary zone that's linked to them. If you have a separate cooktop and oven, the oven can be even farther afield, but be sure there's a surface close by where you can rest anything heavy and hot, such as a steaming casserole.

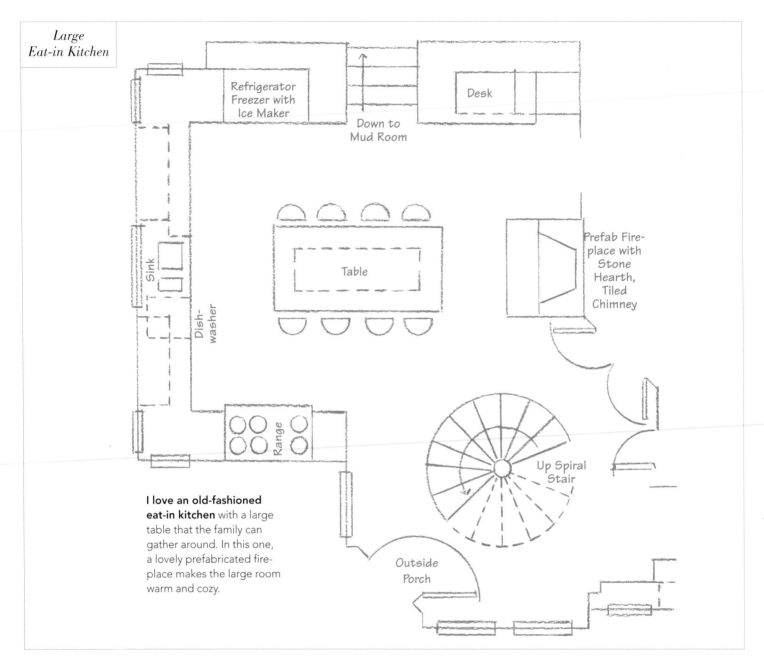

Large
Eat-in Kitchen

Refrigerator Freezer with Ice Maker

Desk

Down to Mud Room

Sink

Dish-washer

Table

Range

Prefab Fireplace with Stone Hearth, Tiled Chimney

Up Spiral Stair

I love an old-fashioned eat-in kitchen with a large table that the family can gather around. In this one, a lovely prefabricated fireplace makes the large room warm and cozy.

Outside Porch

The sink is the busiest place in the kitchen, and it has a lot of attendant accessories: sponges, scrubbies, soaps, brushes, dish drainers, dish towels, and so forth. For me, the sink area is too active for an island and too messy. If I'm feeding the kids breakfast or lunch, I don't want cleanser and water spraying onto the countertop as I'm cleaning up and they are eating.

By contrast, my cooktop is usually clean and clear, accessorized with only a kettle, which looks decorative. Given the question of whether to put the sink or the cooktop in an island, I'd say the cooktop.

WHERE TO BEGIN?

Shop for appliances first, advises Paulette Gambacorta, a designer with Bilotta Kitchens in Mamaroneck, New York. If you don't know what you want before you start developing a plan, you will end up doing your layout twice because appliance preferences and sizes drive the design of the kitchen.

This calls for assessing whether you want more than one oven (what size and type, wall or integrated with the cooktop), a separate cooktop with or without options such as a grill or griddle, a built-in wok, a warming drawer, a microwave, and so forth. Plus, you'll have to decide whether you need a refrigerator and a separate freezer or modular (drawer-size) units. There are so many options with today's appliances that you have to do a lot of "window shopping" to get the big picture. Besides, you don't want to find out about a feature that you would have chosen had you known about it before you made your purchases.

Organizing Your Thoughts

Leave yourself sufficient time for planning. Paulette advises allowing a month before you even order your cabinets. Delivery of stock cabinets can take from three to four weeks, and custom cabinets may take from eight to twelve weeks for delivery. So start planning now. As you do, consider what you like and don't like about your present kitchen. Don't just think about aesthetics, but evaluate the way you work in the room, the floor plan, the steps you take, and your storage needs.

As for style, the best place to begin is with whatever idea you may already have in mind. For me, there is a picture of a kitchen cabinet in my house file that waits for the day I have the time and money. You could begin with one wish-list element: a stone counter or a type of flooring that you've always wanted. This first aesthetic decision

A stone countertop or a tile backsplash can be your wish-list item.

will be a starting-off point for all the others, making them easier to reach. For me, I have to find floor and countertop materials that work with those cabinets I want. If your dream kitchen has a handsome stone countertop, begin with that; then look for a cabinet style, countertop, and flooring to match.

Personal taste matters. I can't determine that for you, but I will give you guidelines regarding wear and tear, ease of maintenance, function, and the relative costs of various options. If you are unsure of what you like, paging through magazines is always a good place to begin. Once you have used the guidelines in this chapter to edit your choices and narrow the field, making decisions will be a snap.

Arts and Crafts style inspired these cabinets.

Blue-stain wood cabinets look elegant here.

CABINETS SET THE STYLE

Cabinets are the real furniture of a kitchen, making their selection both an aesthetic and functional choice. They are also likely to account for the largest portion of the budget. Here's a great money-saving trick: buy off-the-shelf cabinets from a home center, and customize them with strips of wood or decorative molding. I hate it when cabinets just end without any kind of flourish. They need some point of termination. Be careful, though: one client's husband got so carried away at the lumberyard, his wife had to point out that the molding he picked was $3 per linear foot. She added it up, and the total came to $1,500. That got his attention, and it saved the couple from making their kitchen cabinets not only too expensive but also too busy-looking. Don't overdo it.

If your existing cabinets are sound but flat and featureless, new trim can be applied to the doors or frames to dress them up. You can even find kits with precut ornamental pieces and self-adhesive backing.

Hardware can be replaced for a simple spruce-up. And most cabinets can be painted or resurfaced.

Cabinet Face-Lift. If you aren't getting a new kitchen, retrofit existing cabinets. I have. Mine are 30 years old. Would I have chosen them? No. But they are made from oak with a raised-wood panel; sturdy, and the bill to replace them was staggering. I priced replacement:

$28,000! So, we added decorative moldings. The lower molding strip also serves as a handy valance to camouflage the fluorescent strips we installed under the wall units. We also retrofitted the interiors for better storage. At the same time, we added a couple of new cabinets and re-stained all of them in dark walnut. Would I have liked new cabinets? Sure. Do these look good? Yes.

Custom cabinets can be built to your kitchen's specifications.

Am I satisfied? You bet. And the total cost was $2,000, which allowed me to make other changes in the room.

What Are Cabinets Made Of?

Cabinets can be constructed of wood, plastic laminate (a high-quality, thick particleboard underneath a laminate facing), metal (practically obsolete in residential installations), or stainless steel, an option I would never recommend, however. It's cold and shows smudges.

Laminate. There are different brands and grades of plastic laminate, but cabinets made from this material generally are the least expensive you can buy. For the most part, they are devoid of detail and frameless, so don't look for raised panels, moldings, or inlaid beads on plastic laminate cabinets.

Although the surface is somewhat vulnerable (depending on the quality) to scratches and chips, plastic laminate cabinets can be refaced relatively inexpensively. Laminates come in a formidable range of colors and patterns. Some of the newer speckled and patterned designs, which now even include denim and canvas, not only look great but won't show minor scratches and scars.

Wood. Wood cabinets offer the greatest variety of type, style, and finish. *Framed* cabinets (the full frame across the face of the cabinets may show between the doors)

are popular for achieving a traditional look, but they are slightly less roomy inside. That's because you lose the width of the frame, which can be as much as an inch, on each side. *Frameless* cabinets have full overlay doors and drawer fronts. With frameless cabinets, you gain about 2 inches of interior space per cabinet unit. Multiply that by the number of cabinet doors or drawer units you have, and add it up. It's easy to see that if space is at a premium, choose the frameless or full-overlay type. Besides, most cabinet companies now offer enough frameless styles to give you a traditional look in cabinetry, if that's your style.

Analyze your storage needs before buying cabinets.

The Decorative Aspect of Cabinets

While the trend in overall kitchen style is toward more decorative moldings and carvings, the trend in cabinet doors is toward simpler designs. Plain panels, for instance, are now more popular than raised panels. They allow you to have more decoration elsewhere. Ornamentation is effective when it is used to provide a focal point over a hood, fridge, or sink. Instead of installing a single crown profile, you might create a three- or four-piece crown treatment, or add a carving of grapevines, acanthus leaves, or another decorative motif. In the traditional kitchen, add them, but sparingly.

Finishes. Of all of the choices you will need to make regarding wood cabinets, the selection of the finish may be the hardest. Wood can be stained, pickled, painted, or oiled. Your selection will be determined in part by whether you order stock or custom cabinets. Finishing options on stock cabinets are usually limited, and variations are offered as an upgrade. Translation: more money.

A light wood finish looks informal and brightens a room.

A dark wood finish is formal and adds traditional style.

*"Try working with stock cabinets.
They cost less and speed up the process."*

Try working with the manufacturer's stock cabinets. It not only costs less but also speeds up the process. There is usually a reason why manufacturers offer certain woods in certain choices: it's because those choices work best with other elements in the room.

Wood Stains. Today, stains that are close to natural wood tones are popular, particularly darker woods with natural wood finishes. Cherry is quickly becoming the number-one wood in the country. Pickled finishes, very popular in the early 1990s, are now looking dated. Some woods, particularly oak, have more grain than others. Some, such as maple, are smoother. And others, such as birch, dent and ding more easily. The quality and inherent characteristics of the wood you choose will help determine whether it is better to stain, pickle, or paint. For staining, you need a good-quality clear wood. Pickling, because it has pigment in the stain, masks more of the grain but is still translucent. Because paint completely covers the grain, painted wood cabinets are usually made of lesser-quality paint-grade wood.

Grain Pattern. Be careful choosing wood with a lot of grain in a natural finish. Kitchens automatically have a lot of horizontal and vertical lines. Consider that, and look at an oak floor to understand that you could end up with a battle of textures and patterns. Oak has a cathedral-shaped grain. Pine does not stain well. In addition, maple can come in strips that are uneven in color, giving cabinets a striped look of darker and lighter bands.

Ask for a full-size cabinet door sample to see how a wood finish looks made up. Don't worry about the door style at this point. This sample will give you a sense of wood quality and composition. Your cabinet vendor will either have one or be able to get one for you at no cost.

WATCH OUT FOR WHITE CABINETS

The painted white cabinet is still a classic and will always have its place. But generally the completely white kitchen is gone. Now, if you have white kitchen cabinets, they are combined with a wood floor, a stone countertop, or a patterned backsplash to add warmth to the room. Whites tend to yellow, and bright, arctic, polar whites show the yellowing even more. I prefer a softer, more forgiving white. Different whites have varying casts, such as pink-white, gray-white, or yellow-white, and the cast of the white you choose should be reflected in your choices of countertop, trim, and other painted surfaces.

Wood darkens with age. In addition, color intensifies when there is more of it. A small sample doesn't truly reflect the depth of a room full of vertical cabinets. So if you're deciding between two slight variations, go with lighter.

The graining that can lead to pattern clutter is also what makes wood so forgiving and therefore long lasting. As with laminate patterns, the wood's grain pattern conceals dings, gouges, and chips.

Painted Wood. Paint gives wood a smooth, clean finish. You can paint when you want a change or if the finish starts to show wear. This comes at no small expense, though, because the painter will have to sand the surfaces well before applying several coats of paint. If you choose painted cabinets, be sure to obtain a small can of the exact same paint from your kitchen vendor. There is usually a charge for this, but it allows you to do small touch-ups yourself, ridding your cabinets of particularly hideous scars without a complete repainting. While in theory the color choice for painted cabinets is infinite, manufacturers generally offer four shades of white and a few other standard color options from which to choose.

Pickled Wood. Pickled cabinets fall midway between full-grain natural cabinets and painted ones. Pickling is a combination of stain and paint, allowing some of the grain to show. It subdues the strongest patterns, while it covers over the lesser ones. The degree depends on your choice and on the options available from the manufacturer.

Painted wood cabinets provide a nice contrast to the natural-wood floor.

Hardware. Handles are easier to maneuver than knobs. Advocates of universal design, which takes into consideration the capabilities of all people — young and old, with and without physical limitations — recommend them. Knobs do not work easily for children, people with arthritis, or anyone else. A handle with a backplate will keep fingerprints off the cabinet door.

FITTING CABINETS INTO YOUR LAYOUT

This calls for attention to the kitchen layout. In specifying cabinets, first let common sense and budget be your guide. How do you live? How much do you cook? How complicated are your meals? Kitchen geography can help you determine how much storage you need and where it should be. Mentally divide your kitchen into zones: food preparation, food consumption, and so on. If you do paperwork in the kitchen, repot your plants and start seeds, or work on a hobby, add a place for that into your layout, too. Use islands to separate functions.

The Island. A kitchen workhorse, the island, is not new to kitchen design. It's as old as the solid, slightly elevated, central table of medieval kitchens in England. But it was only a worktop. Today, it's kitchen geography: it divides the room into separate tasks and also creates areas of

function, such as food preparation and cleanup, eating, and socializing. The peninsula can serve the same purpose.

How Tall Is Too Tall?

Upper cabinets are typically 12 inches deep; base, or lower, cabinets are 24 inches deep. With the exception of a desk unit, standard base cabinets are always the same height, 36 inches. Although I like to keep clean lines and planes as much as possible, some circumstances call for variations in the height of lower cabinets. There may be an often-used area where you want a countertop at which you can work while seated, for example.

This kitchen's roomy central island provides a place to eat and socialize.

Upper cabinets come in two or three standard heights: 30, 36, and 42 inches. The 30-inch ones look short; 36-inch cabinets look standard, and 42-inch ones can look too tall if your ceiling is not unusually high. In general, there is a slight up-charge for 30-inch cabinets and a big jump in price for 42-inch units. Anything else is double custom, and you don't want to go there. You don't need to, either. For greater variation, upper cabinets can be installed at varying heights. The old standard was to install 30-inch upper cabinets under a soffit—the often, but not always, boxed-in area just under the ceiling and above the wall cabinets. Now, unless you have very tall ceilings, soffits are practically obsolete. Provided you have standard-height, 8-foot ceilings, the way to go now seems to be 36-inch cabinets with the remaining space of 6 inches or so filled with

I used tall windows to break up a large bank of upper cabinets.

decorative trim up to the ceiling. It is a nicer, more refined look than cabinets that extend all the way to the ceiling, unless you prefer something contemporary and totally sleek and without ornament.

Size and Space. You don't want a massive bank of cabinets, either. Add up the dimensions wherever you're considering wall units. The counter is 36 inches high; backsplashes typically range from 15 to 17 inches. So with 36-inch-high upper cabinets, we're talking 7 1/2 feet in all, 8 feet if you chose 42-inch-high wall units. Your own size can help determine which ones to choose. Determine what's comfortable by measuring your reach. A petite person will lose access to the top third of a cabinet. An inch or two can make a very big difference.

Also, be sure that the small appliances you keep on the countertop fit under the wall cabinets. Having them sit at the front edge of a countertop is an accident waiting to happen. A lot of people who have "appliance garages" discovered this. Whenever they pulled out the appliance, which places it nearer the counter's edge, they watched their mixer or coffeemaker tumble to the floor.

Often people need extra storage, so they extend the cabinets up to the ceiling. This provides the added extra storage space, but it can only be reached by a step stool. An open soffit above the upper cabinets provides just as much space for oversize, infrequently used objects, and it

is equally accessible by stepladder. Plus it can be both a display area and perfect home for hard-to-store items: pitchers, trays, salad bowls, vases, collectibles, platters, covered servers, and so forth.

For variety, mix glass- and solid-door upper cabinets.

Soffits and Ceilings. Some people hate open soffits and see them as dust and grease collectors. While this is somewhat true, it isn't an insurmountable problem, especially when you consider that cabinets that extend to the ceiling are much more costly. If the thought of a soffit as a grease-sleeve bothers you, consider boxing in the space. If you love to display collectibles or pretty pieces, leave the soffit open. Just be sure it is of meaningful size. While

An open soffit can be left clear or used to display a collection. If you use a soffit as a display area, light it properly.

A freestanding hutch can serve as a message center.

kitchen desk. Instead, they use it as the family message center and generally stand or perch on a stool. An additional, taller counter simply introduces more clutter to a room that is already overburdened with paraphernalia. And forget a desk-high cabinet, too. Instead use a standard counter-height cabinet to streamline whenever and wherever you can in the room.

Think about outfitting the desk area with a phone and answering machine and a corkboard for notes, your family's social schedule, invitations, and reminders. If you have room, a file drawer makes sense for storing school and business papers that need to be easy to retrieve. Also, if you don't have a separate study, and there's room, the kitchen may be a place to keep

mail-slot-size soffits will collect grease, they will not display anything of size or proportion—a failure on two fronts. In addition, when a soffit is narrow, it looks dark.

the family computer. Not only will you likely be using it more in the future for household record-keeping, but you can also help the kids with their homework and monitor their Internet use.

The Kitchen Desk

Here is some advice about the desk cabinet. Feedback from my customers is that they never really sit at the

A Niche for the TV. Many people also want a TV in the kitchen. Plan for it. Who wants to see the back of the set or look at cords stretching across work areas, atop the refrigerator or the stove? Space and an outlet can be built into the lower portion of a well-placed wall cabinet or an open unit. Just remember to allow plenty of room for air to circulate around the TV.

STORAGE SOLUTIONS: BEHIND CLOSED DOORS

Thank goodness everyone has stopped asking for the flip-down soap/sponge holder. I found them next to useless. Most were too small to hold as many sponges as I use. Nothing ever dried inside that stuffy little place, which created a breeding ground for bacteria. (As we all now know, sponges must be left to dry overnight.) Worse, soap and water would run down the inside of the cabinet door; the trays would rust; they were hard to clean; and everything around this gimmicky gadget would get all scummy. Even though I hate them, if your sink is in an island, tilt-top soap trays can make a sensible home for the sponge. The best are made with a stainless-steel lining that is removable for cleaning.

But there are many storage options that are extremely useful that I can recommend. At the top of the list is a spice drawer or rack attached to an upper cabinet or door. Both drawer and door spice racks are offered as factory options when you order cabinets, or you can retrofit them into existing cabinets. They provide visible access to all spices, so you don't end up, as I do, with

three tins of cinnamon, nine jars of garlic salt, four tiny bottles of vanilla, and no red pepper.

Lazy Susans

These rotating trays make items in the back of corner cabinets accessible. I also put very inexpensive, plastic lazy Susans in a small upper cabinet. Wonderful! Love them. My salt, pepper, sugar, and other seasonings

This built-in unit holds cookbooks and has slots for organizing mail.

all spin and rotate and are visible and easy for me to reach now. I'm having so much fun. Who knew I had five cans of cooking spray?

Pie-cut door attachments can provide the same accessibility as a lazy Susan. (See the illustrations below.) Your choice depends on how much and what kind of storage you need. My corner cabinet is home to

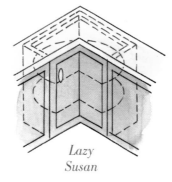

Lazy Susan

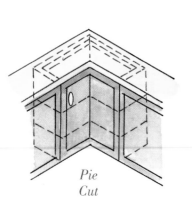

Pie Cut

sodas, chips, and cooking materials, so I have a pie-cut. A lazy Susan is more stable, best for pots, bowls, and larger, heavier objects.

Pull-Outs, Roll-outs, and Dividers

Pull-out fittings maximize the use of very narrow spaces. There are just two options for these areas: vertical tray-storage units or a pull-out pantry. I have a 12-inch-wide base cabinet that was turned into a pull-out pantry with storage on the door, as well as inside. I keep my teas, coffees, soups, beans, and all kinds of stuff there. I've gotten a huge return on this pull-out pantry investment.

Pull-out racks for cabinets and lid-rack dividers for drawers are also available from some cabinet suppliers. They are handy, but if you have enough cabinet storage space, the best thing is to store pots and pans with the lids on them in a couple of large cabinets.

I designed this cutlery drawer for a client.

Roll-out cabinets are great and offer a lot of flexibility. They are adjustable to accommodate bulky countertop appliances and stock pots, and they can save a lot of steps and banging around. If you have a lot of ding marks inside your cabinets and on your big pots and pans, you'll know what I mean.

I have divided another base cabinet vertically into separate parts. (See below.) Some of the vertical spaces are further subdivided horizontally. That's where I store cutting boards, cookie trays, baking tins, and big glass

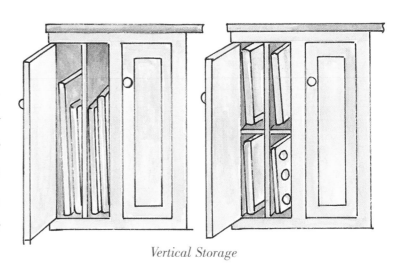

Vertical Storage

Space above the cooktop displays trays here.

interior of the drawer. They are as bad as bookshelves spread too far apart. I like *cutlery dividers* that are almost no wider than a spoon, and I want separate sections for teaspoons, cereal spoons, breakfast and dinner knives, lunch forks, dinner forks, and serving pieces. Because one of my sons will eat only with plastic utensils, he must have another section. Add to this a section for miscellaneous utensils such as spoons for iced tea, chopsticks, and so on. Drawer dividers should be adjustable in case your needs, or your cutlery, change.

Knife, Towel, and Bread Storage. For similar reasons, I don't like carving-knife inserts. There's always one too many knives or a knife that won't fit. If you want a place to store knives, use slotted storage on a countertop. Frequently islands have false backs because they are deeper than base cabinets. Slots for knives can be cut into the area of the countertop that covers the void behind the base cabinet.

baking dishes. These units should not be too wide because, when loaded, they are very heavy.

Chef's pantries, as they are called, with racks on the doors, look great in the catalogs but provide limited storage. They offer nothing for storing large-size items.

Other Organizers

I have a gripe with the cutlery drawers provided by kitchen cabinet manufacturers. They are always too big and too clumsy, and they fail to take advantage of the full

A pull-out towel bar? I've never had one, but it seems like a good idea. I have an actual towel bar mounted at the end of my island for dish towels to dry. I never had a bread-drawer either. A friend asked about the red metal box on my kitchen counter. "Looks like an old bread box," she said. "What do you keep in it?" You guessed it: bread, bagels, and muffins. It works for me, and because my kids live on the three-bagel diet, it's perfect.

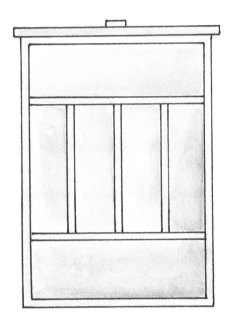

A Divided Cutlery Drawer

The Much-touted Appliance Garage. First of all, the tambour door frequently gets stuck, which is maddening. There are units with flip-up or pocket doors that work better. If you have a corner where the space between the upper and lower cabinets runs the full length of the refrigerator, pantry, or wall-oven, an appliance garage can bridge the transition nicely. However, it eliminates a lot of countertop, usually where that surface is most needed.

You can obtain all these storage options at the time you buy your cabinets. But you don't have to and may not even want to until you see how you really end up using your kitchen. I added storage amenities as the need arose and the idea seized me. A carpenter or handyman can often make them or install off-the-shelf units as I did. My latest is a felt-lined box for the dining room server, to hold my sterling serving pieces. I just went to a local woodworker with measurements, and he is making it up just the way I want it.

Think outside of the box. We get in a rut; it is hard to be objective. Ask friends where they keep their kitchen stuff, and analyze every aspect of how you use your kitchen. Store things at point of use: leftover containers and sandwich bags near the refrigerator; mixing bowls and carving knives near the sink.

GARBAGE & RECYCLING

Garbage and recycling take up lot of space and should be kept out of sight but easy to reach for use. With a family of six, only a large garbage pail will do. Mine is mounted in an 18-inch-wide base cabinet. My friend, Linda, got two tiny, toy-size bins. She has a preschooler, and both bins are full by 10 A.M.

With a diabetic son, we go through lots of sugar-free soda because juices are not allowed. So I have another large pull-out recycling bin for cans, and a third, smaller unit for other metal and tin recycling. An alternative is to stack two good-size units, one behind the other, full base-cabinet height.

Get the pull-out waste receptacles that operate at the drawer-pull and don't require a two-step motion. And avoid those small garbage-bag inserts that flip out from under the sink cabinet.

APPLIANCES

If cabinets set the style of your kitchen, appliances rule over its major functions. The appliances are the core of the room, and their selection is among the most important decisions you will make. They deserve serious thought and research. Appliances are big-ticket items with which you'll be living for many years. So think about your appliance needs in terms of your current lifestyle and how that may or may not change over the course of the next dozen years. If your kids are going off to college in a year or two, will you need a large-capacity refrigerator? Conversely, if your family is young and growing, maybe you need a larger refrigerator than you currently use.

Good-quality appliances are often conspicuous for what they don't do: specifically, make noise. Choose dishwashers that whisper, oven hoods that don't roar, and refrigerators that don't hum loudly. Other obvious variables to take into account are the size of your kitchen, the size of your budget, and the size of your family. Also think about your lifestyle. Is yours a two-career household, more likely to heat something in a microwave than prepare complete meals? How often do you entertain— and how many people do you usually invite for dinner or parties? What kind of food do you cook? Do you need simple appliances or a flexible range of sturdy workhorses that will be constantly in use?

Most homeowners are obsessed with their appliances. It's a worthwhile obsession, except that it sometimes centers more on looks than function.

Appliances drive the functionality of a kitchen. Choose them first— before making other decisions.

Modular units, such as separate ovens and cooktop, allow flexibility in the room's layout.

Cookers That Can Stand the Heat

The choices in ovens and cooktops have proliferated and expanded significantly in recent years. Your first consideration will be your heating preference: Gas or electric? As a general rule, I suggest gas cooktops over electric ones. Electric cooktops are slow to heat up and slower to cool down. As a result, when you switch settings from high to low, response time is sluggish and the meal can burn. Gas cooktops respond immediately; temperatures change the moment the setting is switched. Equally important, gas burners usually provide a broad, progressive range of settings between low and high, while electric plates have more limited ranges, sometimes as few as three.

Different criteria apply to ovens, where I prefer electric to gas because electric provides more-even heat. Gas ovens with jets at the rear generate hot zones, hottest at the top, less so at the bottom. In the hands of an expert, this can be used effectively to cook different dishes at the same time. For most of us, however, the even heat from electricity ensures a better outcome, particularly for baking and roasting. Electric fan convection ovens, rather than conventional radiant electric ovens, work best because they produce rich golden brown roasts that are appealing to the eye as well as the palate.

Contiguous grates let you slide a pot smoothly across the cooking surface.

Separate or Together? Next, decide if you want a range that integrates the oven and cooktop or if you prefer separate appliances for each. In small kitchens, you may not have a choice. I vote to separate the cooktop and oven whenever possible. It gives the room a sleeker, more uniform look. The kitchen is such a busy place, so full of activity that I think every opportunity should be taken to streamline. The old-fashioned stove creates an ugly break in cabinets and countertops. Not only do separate wall ovens provide a svelte built-in appearance, they also make it easier to check on the food while it's

PREVENTING & CLEANING UP MESSES

Cooktops with continuous grates allow you to heat up an area that is larger than a single burner. With no crevices or breaks between the cooktop and the countertop, they also make cleanup easy. So do sealed burners. They cost more but are worth the investment. In redesigning Regis Philbin's Connecticut kitchen, I noticed that the burners were both small and high. When his wife, Joy, who's a wonderful cook and hostess, slid a pasta-sauce pot to the side, it fell off the tall small burner. Lesson? Choose good-size burners with smooth, contiguous grates.

Many gas and electric ovens are either self-cleaning or continuous-cleaning. Their interiors are coated with a substance that literally burns stains and spills away at high temperatures, but the coating will be harmed if you clean your oven with harsh cleansers or chemical oven cleaners.

WHERE THERE IS SMOKE . . .

Adequate ventilation is necessary for any cooking system; the most effective is vented outdoors. A fan is not enough. You need a hooded system (pictured left) over the cooktop to remove smoky, greasy, smelly air that will otherwise ruin your surfaces and leave a stale cooking odor in the room. Hoods can be wall mounted, cantilevered over a range, or installed above islands or peninsulas. Most of them also contain additional features, such as lighting and infrared plate-warming lamps. They come in a wide variety of standard sizes and finishes. At greater expense, you can have one custom designed.

CFM, which stands for cubic feet per minute, is the air-movement rating given to a vent hood in operation. Hoods made of wood are limited to 1,100 CFM, while stainless-steel hoods have ratings that can go to 1,300 or 1,400 CFM and even higher in commercial versions. This extra power is important to a serious cook who may be using professional equipment such as a wok or a grill insert. Furthermore, a stainless-steel hood is the easiest to clean, especially when it hasn't been covered with heavy ornamentation, which is a repository for grease and grime.

Many new ranges are self-ventilating and have a downdraft system that forces greasy air through a filter and then moves it through ductwork to the outdoors. But remember that the longer the duct run, the more power the fan will need to be efficient. As with other appliances, the best vent hoods are the quietest ones. Ask the salesperson about the unit's noise rating.

cooking and get it in and out of the oven. Besides, it's unpleasant enough when you have to stand and stir a hot pot of something without having to endure added heat emanating from the oven.

Whether your cooktop is part of the range or separate, there are many options in stovetop cooking alone. A standard cooktop has four burners, and the average household may need nothing more complex. Increasingly, however, manufacturers are offering six burners and modular accessories such as griddles, grills, rotisseries, barbecues, kebab cookers, deep fryers, or woks. It's up to your cooking style and your budget.

Speeding Up the Cooking Process. Convection ovens cook faster than conventional ovens and slower than microwaves. Like microwaves, they call for adjustments in your recipes. The heating element is behind, rather than inside, the oven, and a fan circulates heated air. Cooking occurs by the forced air rather than the heating element. Convectioned chocolate chip cookies are not as moist as ones cooked the old-fashioned way.

New units combine microwave and convection cooking technologies in a single oven. These super-quick ovens can roast a whole chicken in just 20 minutes. And it comes out moist and browned. Do you have to learn to cook all over again? No. Computer chips in these new models convert the conventional cooking time for you.

Consider Interior Oven Size. Even if you only use the oven at Thanksgiving and Christmas, it will have to accommodate a good-size bird. If you never prepare such major meals, smaller may do. Wall ovens are available in a wider range of size options than ranges that include both the oven and cooktop. There are ranges that now offer two ovens (one is small while the other is standard size) that can roast or bake different parts of the meal at different temperatures. So if your kitchen can't accommodate a pair of wall ovens, and you cook large meals or entertain often, this is a convenient option for you.

A slim-line refrigerator is flush with the cabinets.

Stepping Up to the Pros

Committed cooks, lavish entertainers, and large families with even larger kitchens may want to consider commercial equipment. Commercial ranges offer higher heat and contain six burners or more and ovens with lots of space, often with zones that allow simultaneous cooking of different dishes at different temperatures.

I love the look of stainless steel, but I hate the fact that I'm constantly wiping fingerprints and smudges off the doors.

Commercial stoves, which are always gas-fired, offer more than a lot of space. Because they are built to higher standards than their residential brethren, they have an astonishingly long life. In this era of planned obsolescence, they can last through 30 to 40 years of constant use.

Yet, while everyone loves commercial-looking appliances, don't succumb to the temptation to overbuy. If you want the look and maybe just a little of the extra firepower, professional-*style* equipment is an alternative.

Refrigerators: *Think Slim & Flush*

For reasons of both appearance and function, I have a strong bias for slim-line refrigerators that are flush with the front of the cabinets. Their shallowness, like a built-in cooktop, keeps them from intruding into the room and interrupting the line of the cabinetry. It also keeps food from getting lost. Who needs moldy leftovers that are left behind the cold cuts in a refrigerator that's more than 2 feet deep?

I have a 48-inch side-by-side slim-line model. The side-by-side is the least energy-efficient of three options, which

This commercial refrigerator consumes a lot of energy.

also include freezer on the bottom (bottom-mount) or freezer on the top (top-mount). The advantage of a side-by-side unit is its narrower doors. They don't swing too far into the room. When your husband is stationed in front of an open refrigerator door contemplating the contents, you can still get by him.

The Reviews Are In. I'm always hearing raves about bottom-mount models. One customer of mine says her family likes the wide shelves with everything in the refrigerator compartment conveniently at eye-level. Freezers, like ovens, are used infrequently, so this arrangement makes sense for many. Another good idea is a modular freezer drawer, which you can install into a bank of cabinets or into an island or peninsula. It's not at all inconvenient. Just the opposite. Locate it where it gets used. If it's for the kids' frozen yogurt, put it where they can get access to it. I installed one for clients in Maine, and they love it. You can buy modular refrigerator drawers, as well. Keep the produce where you rinse and chop it.

Dishwashers

Try one on for size. Customers always ask me what dishwasher is best. It's a question that I often ask at appliance stores. Most often, the answer is "whichever one you want," or "they're all good."

Okay, maybe they all wash dishes pretty well, but there are other key issues to

A bottom-mount refrigerator (at the far right) is efficient.

consider. My everyday stem-footed glasses, for instance, are too tall for the upper portion of my dishwasher, and my fine china doesn't fit into the lower portion either. So, I think it is worth the effort to take your dishes to the appliance store and try out the dishwasher's fit for you. Or buy a model with adjustable racks.

Today's dishwashers have other added features you may or may not want. They all affect the cost, so be sure you want the extra features. For example, if you have good china and fine stemware, you need a unit that will treat them gently. More options include convection drying, concealed controls, custom front panels, a built-in water softener, delayed-start mechanisms, modular drawer-size units, as well as others. Do some home-work, and shop around to find something that suits the way you live.

Noise is another important dishwasher consideration, depending on your home's layout. I usually run the dishwasher as I'm leaving the kitchen, and even if I stay there for a while, I'm usually in clean-up mode, not reading and relaxing mode. But if a noisy dishwasher bothers you, new models run quieter, some practically in silence.

EVERYTHING ABOUT THE KITCHEN SINK

Sinks are proof-positive that there is fashion to everything. Thirty years ago, people couldn't wait to get rid of their oversized porcelain sinks. Today, they are back in style, especially the old-fashioned farm style with the exposed

With a high-arc faucet you don't need a deep sink.

apron. Given my druthers, I prefer one oversized bowl to two. With two, I never know which one to use, and I'm always transferring things from one sink bowl to the other. I like lots of room in a sink, but not necessarily in two compartments.

I don't like the sink being too deep, either. Eight to 9 inches is usually sufficient for filling big pasta pots. With a 12-inch-deep sink, you will break your back leaning over it. Big sinks take up a lot of cabinet and counter area, so you sacrifice surface and storage when you install one. If you need more, consider two separate sinks (as opposed to a multiple-bowl sink), each one a different size and located where you're most apt to use it. I prefer one big sink for cleanup and a second, smaller one for chopping vegetables and disposal.

It's nice if you can position the sink so that it extends out a bit from the standard 24-inch-deep cabinets. This not only changes the plane to provide visual variety and a bit more room on the deck for a faucet, it also makes it easier to clean the detritus that collects in the area behind the sink.

Sink Materials

Stainless-steel sinks have some good things going for them and some not so good. They are totally watertight and heat resistant. They also provide a softer landing when a butterfingers like me drops something. Furthermore, they are versatile and look good in vintage and period kitchens, as well in contemporary-style settings. A heavy-gauge stainless-steel sink of good quality will hold up against dings, dents, and scratches for years, especially if it has a brushed finish. To keep it looking good, clean it with a nonabrasive cleanser.

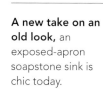

A new take on an old look, an exposed-apron soapstone sink is chic today.

The sinks we call porcelain are really *enamel over cast iron*. Enamel is more expensive than stainless steel, and if you drop a glass, the glass will probably shatter. (The better the stemware, the more certain it will break.)

There are also *enameled steel* (versus cast iron) sinks, and they are the cheapest option. They chip easily, make noise when hit, and break glasses and dishes. If you want to know what they'll look like in a couple of years, just think of a two-week-old manicure. Worse, the steel under the enamel is black, making every chip glaringly apparent.

SINK INSTALLATION

For sinks, you have a choice of a drop-in or undermount installation. That choice is usually dictated by the type of countertop material you select. An undermounted sink is installed from beneath the cabinet. It has no rim. Undermounted sinks are typically paired with countertops made of any solid-surfacing material or stone.

A drop-in sink is self-rimmed. It is literally dropped into a precisely cut hole in the countertop that supports it. This type usually works best for plastic laminate, wood, and tile countertops.

An integral sink is fabricated from the same material as the countertop, which can be stone or a solid-surfacing material. The sink and countertop appear to be one smooth, seamless piece.

Sinks made of *solid surfacing* (a color-through plastic laminate) are prefabricated, usually by a certified installer. They are expensive. And while I acknowledge that they are very sanitary and very tough and durable, they look too bland for me.

Marble, slate, and *soapstone* are additional options. Lately I have been using a lot of marble and soapstone sinks, and the clients who have them love them. They are expensive, but they have a wonderful look, and they can be specified in any size, depth, or shape.

The Right Faucet

For many reasons, it's best to choose the faucet and sink at the same time. Most sinks come with precut holes for the plumbing. Make sure yours has the right number of holes for the faucet you choose. My sink has three holes: one for the faucet, one for a soap dispenser, and another for the sprayer. My previous sink had four, and I had to put a stainless-steel plug on the top. Most annoying. You don't have to worry about this if you buy an undermounted sink. You install it from beneath the countertop, so the holes for the faucet are drilled into the countertop, usually behind the sink. However, you can install a faucet on the countertop to the side of the sink or on the backsplash, too.

Keep the size and shape of the sink in mind when choosing a faucet, too. A single rectangular sink can work with almost any faucet and in any configuration. But if you are using a double sink or a sink with bowls of different sizes, you will have to use a single-hole faucet that is set in center, between both sinks.

Regardless of style, I recommend a *single-lever* faucet, in which hot and cold can be mixed to the temperature you want with one hand. With separate handles, water is always either too cold or too hot. Also, to adjust the temperature, you have to put down the vegetables you are washing or the glasses you are rinsing. And these faucets are easiest to operate, especially for older people and kids who may find grabbing and turning a crosshandle design or a knob difficult. Two-handle faucets that are separate from the spout (called a *wide-spread set*) require three holes. A *center set*, which features separate hot and cold water taps and a spout that all seem connected by a bar, typically also require three holes.

I love the look of the two-handled faucets, however, and used one for a brief moment in my last house. I was a young, impressionable girl then. You can bet I did not repeat that mistake in my new house.

COUNTERTOPS & BACKSPLASHES

Choosing countertops and backsplashes is intimidating to a lot of people, and with good reason. There are many options for these surfaces, which are discussed here.

Single-lever faucets are easiest to use.

"Tile countertops are inevitably uneven, although the degree of unevenness depends on whether you choose machine-made tiles or the more rustic handmade ones."

The selection of a countertop material (and many other kitchen surfaces for that matter) depends largely on how much of a neat freak you are. I consider my kitchen to be really clean only when it smells like bleach.

Stone. Marble and granite are in increasing demand for kitchens with a more traditional look. More people are also experimenting with *concrete* formulations, too. Although they are not maintenance-free, they can be sealed and custom-mixed. And, like granite, they develop a surface patina with age and use. This makes for natural variations in wear.

Tile. Tile is inevitably uneven, although the degree of unevenness depends on whether you choose machine-made tiles or the more rustic handmade ones. They are all set in grout, which catches crumbs and bacteria and can discolor, even with a sealer. I would never use tiles that require wide areas of rough grout. It's just too much of a trap for grime.

Stainless Steel. You practically have to wipe stainless steel down with a squeegee every night. Unless yours is a trophy kitchen, created more to be admired than used, I would limit the use of this material to small areas only. Stainless steel also dents and scratches easily.

Wood. Be wary of wood, even butcher block. In certain states, for example, restaurants with wood counters are required by law to have city and state inspections.

Plastic Laminate. This is the least expensive countertop material. And for the most part, you get what you pay for. It chips and scratches. Of course, better grades of plastic laminate hold up longer.

Solid Surfacing Material. With solid color all the way through, this material is triple the price of plastic laminate. However, stains, burns, and scratches can be sanded down and eradicated. In some cases, it's more expensive than stone, but manufacturers say it will last 20 years.

Backsplashes are an area where you can really have fun — sometimes too much fun. People often overdo their backsplashes. Most of the backsplash ends up obscured by what's on the kitchen counter anyway. Use tile, create a mural, but don't go overboard.

A marble countertop can be reserved for the island.

BATHROOMS

When you're redoing a bathroom, sometimes you can get away with **minor repair work** and a **cosmetic makeover**. But the median age of the average American home is now over 25 years, and that's when things such as the roof as well as the shower-stall pan start to go. So will your bathroom require a **complete overhaul** or just a change of look? Are you dreaming of a Sybarite's delight or a **minimalist's spa**? A confection of pink **floral tiles or a rustic tumbled marble** grotto? Once you start fantasizing about the project, it's hard to hold the line sometimes. One customer wanted to update her bathroom without tackling a total redo. Her main wish was for a new **medicine cabinet** with a larger mirror, **better lighting**, and outlets with ground-fault circuit interrupters (GFCIs). This simple request meant we were involving a carpenter to

I used standard tile to fashion a dynamic basketweave-pattern floor for this remodeled Victorian-era bath.

Single-peg rails
installed high on the
walls hold towels
and wraps.

*" . . . address the basic
functionality
of your bathroom. "*

replace the vanity; an electrician for the lighting and new

outlets; a tile man for the work around the new larger

cabinet; a plasterer to touch up the wall around the new

medicine cabinet above the tile; and a painter. Wow!

Even simple bathroom redos (meaning retaining the

existing floor plan and fixtures) involve a lot of trades-

people. So while you're still in the thinking stage, address

the basic functionality of your bathroom. How many

people have to share the room? Does the toilet run

constantly? Are your pipes worn? Is the pan in your

shower leaking? If your bathroom is more than 20 years

old, you may be looking at a major overhaul of the space

and replacing fixtures. But is that really necessary?

**A yellow and
white tile floor**
adds a dollop of
sunshine underfoot.

White bead board
looks fresh and clean
in this remodeled
bath in a house
by the sea.

OLD FIXTURES NEVER DIE— THEY CREATE LANDFILL

How deep will you have to dig into your wallet for the project? Compromises are sometimes possible. I am a patcher and a repairer, but I wouldn't use duct tape to hold my toilet tank top together, either. Essentially, my feeling is if it isn't broken, don't fix it. When we bought our current house, a magazine editor friend asked me what I was going to "do" with my bathroom. I could have gutted it and left all the old stuff at the curb. But with years of college tuition payments on the horizon, I asked myself, would an all-new bathroom function measurably better? Would it provide more storage? Would I be poorer? The answers were No, No, and Yes (by about $20,000). So, we have a beautiful "vintage" bathroom with a double-pedestal sink (one body with two basins or bowls and two faucet sets); separate tub and shower stall; plenty of storage; a wonderful marble-capped privacy wall between tub and toilet; and plentiful good flattering lighting.

What changes did we make? We had a few cracked wall tiles and a leaky shower pan to address. Otherwise, we kept everything else. To camouflage the cracked tile, we painted a climbing vine, "growing" from the crack. As a decorator, I have done this trick more than once. You can buy the paint that can be used on ceramic surfaces in a craft store.

"Essentially, my feeling is if it isn't broken, don't fix it."

The shower pan problem was not as easily resolved. This square pan sits at the bottom of your shower floor, underneath the tile. The tendency is to hope that it is not the pan, because that job calls for ripping out the shower. So first we regrouted, which is a lot easier. Maybe the water is seeping behind the tiles, we thought with fingers crossed. Then, when that bubbly spot on the ceiling of the hall below the bathroom reappeared, we bit the bullet and got a new metal pan and retiled the shower floor and lower portion of the shower wall.

Be Practical. If ever you have to do what we did, I can offer some money-saving suggestions. Before he tackles your shower floor, ask the demolition man if he can keep the tiles intact, so you can reuse them. (You will have to soak the tiles in a solvent that loosens the old adhesive, which you can scrape off with a putty knife.) I would only recommend this for a small area, but it's worth asking. However, if you do have to purchase new tiles, buy extras in case you have to replace a few in the future.

Keep in mind, replacement tiles do not have to match. They can be merely compatible or even a complete contrast to the original ones. Two good examples are a white tile wall with a black-and-white checkerboard tile dado or the lower portion of an emerald-color tiled shower (the pan replacement area) with a garnet- or sapphire-color floor and base molding. The alternative is to retile the entire shower stall, which will cost more money and create more mess.

For my bath, we just replaced the bottom tile runs with new tile that almost matches the original white ones above them. There's no need to obsess over a slight variation in color. It will be barely visible, especially in a shower stall or some other place that isn't obvious, such as the wall just behind the toilet or sink.

Reusing Older Fixtures

Like many bathroom materials, porcelain is not biodegradable. Where will it go when we throw it away? Our children will raise their children on landfills, which is one more reason to patch, repair, and reuse things when it's possible. Old tubs can be resurfaced or reglazed, for

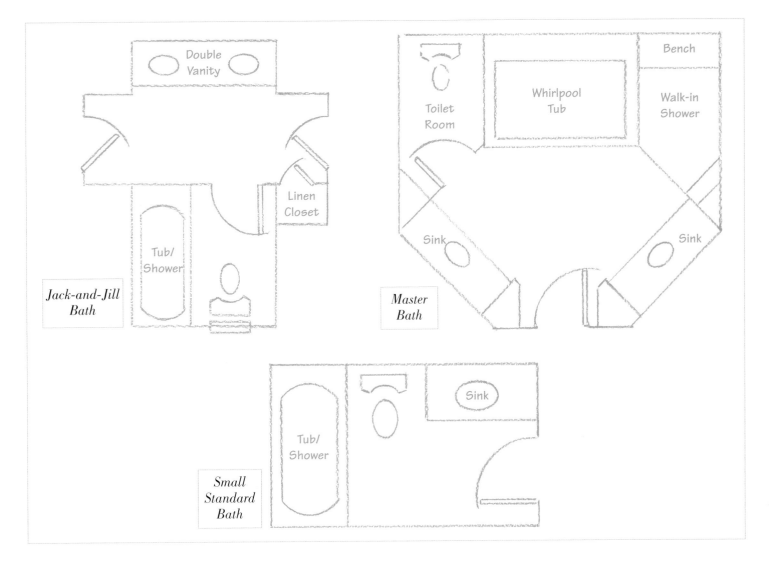

A few strategically placed pictures can camouflage a few replacement tiles in an older bath, left.

Play up the charm of vintage fixtures with a nostalgic wallpaper, right.

example. This really does work, with some limitations. Once you reglaze a tub, you can't use abrasive cleansers on it. And spilled hair dyes and colored bath gels can discolor these materials, so you have to be careful.

If you decide to go for tub resurfacing, always hire a reputable person to do the job. We had a tub in my friend Mollie's guest bath resurfaced and, within a day, the new surface was coming off by the handful in the area around the soap dish. Either the power-washing procedure, which must always be done prior to resurfacing, had missed the spot, or the resurfacers had left standing water in the soap dish, so the new glaze didn't take. From then on, I sought out qualified resurfacing companies, checked referrals, and got a warranty for the job.

Another reason to consider repair versus replacement is that older is better sometimes. When you replace your vintage plumbing fixtures, you will have to make sure that the new stuff conforms to the stricter environmental codes that exist today. For example, old toilets operate on a 3.5-gallon flush. To conserve water, the newer 1.6-gallon flush is now a nationwide standard by federal law. The early low-flush models were poor performers and could only be described as disasters. They never really work on the first try. By having to flush them again and again, are we really saving water? I will concede that although they still don't flush as efficiently as older models, today's low-flush toilets are improving because manufacturers have enlarged and glazed the trap.

Furthermore, old toilets are more sleek and solid looking. Porcelain is expensive, so manufacturers have cut down on the amount used. New-model toilets reveal what is called "the snake" (that's the curved bulge you see on the sides of new toilets) rather than enclosing it in a smooth, porcelain orb as in the past.

Bathroom Inflation

It seems that you can't look at a floor plan of a New York City apartment or a new McMansion without seeing more bathrooms than bedrooms. Although having your own bathroom sounds like a wonderful indulgence, one or more for each person in the house does seem extravagant in relation to construction costs these days. Consider the expenditure in terms of dollars per minute: for the most part, I am in and out of my bathroom each morning in the time it takes to shower and brush my teeth. At night, subtract the shower. Even if you are a complete bathroom dawdler, what percentage of your day do you really spend in there?

Whatever happened to the Jack and Jill bath—that shared space connecting two bedrooms? I think it's time to bring it back. I have two of them in my house. One roomy shared bath with a window is far superior to two stuffy little baths without windows.

SAFETY

Safety has to be a major component in any bathroom design. Most accidents happen at home, and many of them happen in the bathroom. As a matter of fact, a large amount of nursing home admissions occur because of falls, many of which take place in the bath. Falls are a significant cause of death for those over 60. I can't tell you how many times I have heard that an elderly person fell in the shower, broke a hip, and then died due to complications. I don't plan on going that way.

I work with a developer in Palm Beach, and when it comes to the bath, all he wants to show me are trompe l'oeil rosettes, faux marble walls, and other decorations. I want to talk about grab bars and nonskid tile floors. We baby boomers aren't getting any younger. There is a reason why falls are the leading cause of serious bath-

Older toilets use more water, but they flush more completely than new models.

room injuries and usually occur as people are getting into or out of the bathtub or shower. The smooth, glossy surfaces of tubs, showers, and tile get slick when they combine with soap and water. If that surface is a tile floor, there are two things you can do to reduce the hazard. First, install the

Small floor tiles with lots of grout lines provide better traction.

proper type of tile: one that is matte finished and slip resistant. When you're shopping for floor tile, inquire about manufacturers' slip-resistance ratings, which range from 1 to 4; the higher the rating, the less slippery the tile.

Second, use small tiles and wider grout lines. I have a theory about grout and its contribution to safety in wet areas. Grout is usually somewhat gritty, which gives it traction. When wet feet come into contact with smooth tile, they can slip. But the courseness of the grout breaks the skid. Hence, I believe the more grout lines, the less likely you are to fall. I work with a young architect occasionally. He was skeptical about my theory until he slipped in the shower when he was reaching for the shampoo. His shower floor was made up of large tiles that required few grout lines.

Get a Grip

When I built a house for my parents, they were in their early 60s and as healthy as can be. Still, I took certain precautions and used ideas I learned designing for former athletes who suffer from arthritis. Sooner or later, all of these safety precautions have been put to good use. For one thing, I installed grab bars, one by the toilet and another in the shower. Grab bars must be fastened into wall studs or other structural supports. They are invaluable to my dad who has only one leg. Although they are never intended for support, be sure to securely anchor towel rings and bars and soap dishes and shower curtain rods into wall studs just in case someone grabs one to break a fall. My dad fell and took the shower rod down with him. It wasn't anchored; now it is. Breakable, protruding shower or bath fittings, such as porcelain or ceramic soap dishes, can make falls even more dangerous because they can shatter.

The importance of safety features isn't limited to the geriatric set. In high school, my friend fell in the tub and grabbed onto the faucet. It was porcelain and broke into many pieces that severed many nerves in his arm and caused permanent damage.

Safety Doesn't Mean Ugly. Safety features don't have to make your bathroom look like a geriatric ward. I installed a barrier-free shower in my parents' house, which simply means there is no saddle or curb to keep the water in. The floor just tilts so that water drains to the center. Because my dad uses a walker in the shower, this easy-access feature is a must, and the shower actually looks modern and kind of cool. The grab bars resemble beefy towel bars finished in brushed chrome.

In general, I recommend using small tiles in the bathroom with lots of grout in between them. For the shower floor, tiles should be no larger than four inches square. Also avoid loose throw rugs that can skid.

For older people (and we all hope we'll eventually get there), consider other conveniences, such as a toilet that sits high. It's great for my uncle who, prior to hip replacement surgery, couldn't bend easily and had trouble with standard-height or low toilets.

Grab bars are an essential safety feature in any bath.

Compartmentalized spaces make this bathroom, left, efficient and safe for use by more than one person. Note the half-wall that provides privacy for the toilet area. A roof window helps to ventilate the walk-in shower, right.

Make sure all electrical outlets in the bathroom are outfitted with GFCIs. That means that any appliance will shut off automatically if it comes in contact with water while plugged into a GFCI outlet. This is essential where water and electricity are in proximity.

Keep Your Cool. The average hot-water heater is set to heat water to 150 degrees. That's hot enough to cause a third-degree burn on a child's tender skin. If you don't buy a new faucet that comes with a new anti-scald device or pressure-balanced valves to equalize hot and cold water, set your heater at 130 degrees. You will save money and avoid burns.

TILE TALK

The good news about bathrooms is that they are small in most houses and don't require large amounts of materials. Unlike the wallpaper or carpeting for the hall that wanders on and on, you probably don't need a lot of tile for a bathroom. The bad news? The components and materials required to tile the room can be quite expensive and so is the cost of labor to install them. One way to keep the price down is by using standard tile rather than custom or handmade designs.

The labor to install tile costs the same if your tile costs $5 or $25 per square foot. So before you cut back to a less-expensive tile, evaluate the savings against the total bill, rather than just comparing tile versus tile. Not that I am advocating expensive tile! I am a great believer in simplicity when it comes to bathrooms. I am also an advo-

"As my mom says, "When in doubt, do without."

cate of quality and of disrupting your life as infrequently as possible. Do the bathroom right, and do it once.

Though they are considered high end, marble or stone tiles can be less expensive than hand-painted ceramic or some synthetic materials. In a much-used powder room, a stone floor is a wonderful choice. And unlike ceramic, which usually has a smooth surface, stone is mottled, so dirt doesn't show up either. Stone lasts forever and is solid all the way through, so chips and dings won't show.

Extras. Tile costs start to escalate when people add borders, trim and finishing pieces, capping pieces, and raised-relief pieces. Remember, the bathroom is first and foremost a functional space, so be sure to choose components that are appropriate and practical. Too much raised relief creates nesting places for mold and scum. A pitted, rustic country floor adds up to the same problem. While an elegant bath is composed of quality ingredients, more is not necessarily better. Don't over-accessorize. As my mom says, "When in doubt, do without."

Borders

People always ask me where to place a tile border. I think that between 42 and 60 inches from the floor is most visible and, therefore, very effective. That way, the border doesn't get buried behind the toilet, sinks, or tub. Installing a border within that area can also be an effective transition from a tiled surface to the rest of the wall. If your shower is open and visible, continue the border onto the shower walls unless you want to create an entirely different tile design in there. But remember: the lines of the shower are usually different from those in other areas. Shower walls are tall, so you're designing a tile pattern for vertical planes. In other areas of the bathroom, your tile design will usually be for horizontal planes. One simple trick distinguishes a shower. "Frame" the most visible inside wall with a border starting at a point that is one tile in from the edge of the wall. Set the tile inside the border on the diagonal. This creates a dramatic decorative panel that adds depth and dimension to a shower stall.

Walls

In the main area of the bathroom, installing tile from the floor to between 42 and 50 inches up the wall provides ample coverage for splashes generated from the sink, tub, or toilet. In a fully enclosed shower, all the way up the wall works best. You should tile the ceiling of the shower as well. If you don't have an enclosed shower, tile to the top of

A tile border carries out a whimsical theme in this beach bungalow's refurbished bath.

In the shower, the tile border goes higher up on the wall. On the backsplash, the design is lower.

your shower enclosure. Wall, floor, and ceiling tiles won't line up on all four sides of the shower walls, so don't try to force them to. Instead, change the direction or the size of the tiles on the ceiling or floor. Tile installers do not like to put tiles that are larger than 6 inches square on ceilings because of their weight. If a 12-inch tile falls on your head, it will hurt a lot more than if a 4-inch tile falls on you. Wall tiles, on the other hand, can be as large as you like. Of course, they should be in proportion to the size of your room. If you have fallen in love with a 12-inch tile, your tile installer can cut it into smaller sizes for the floor and ceiling, provided there is not too much square footage to cover, which can make the job labor-intensive, thus expensive. In general, I recommend using 6- to 12-inch tile on the wall and 4- to 6-inch tile on the ceiling. Set the ceiling tiles on a diagonal to make the room look larger.

Floors

People often design elaborate floor patterns based on borders and cornerstones and inlays, only to discover that they always keep a bath mat or a throw rug on the floor. Only in an entry area or toilet room, where you don't use a bath mat, does a pattern make sense. It's best if the design extends over the entire area and has a finishing border to terminate it. Be sure that the design sits far enough out from the

For a house in Maine, I created a simple tile floor pattern with a border that doesn't get lost under the vanity.

This marble countertop was made from one slab of stone.

toekick of your vanity to be visible. This usually means locating it a minimum of 3 inches out from the toekick if the vanity is built in.

Keep It Simple. For example, be aware of what a large expanse of the tiles will look like. A client, Linda, recently had marble tile installed in her large master bath and was shocked by the patchwork effect. Some tiles are tight and densely speckled. Others have large blemishes and 6-inch freckles. The distinctive markings that made a single tile handsome were too busy for an entire wall of tiles. If you're going with stone, choose a quiet pattern that has uniform markings. When you're at the showroom or home center, ask to see samples of the extremes that a particular stone is apt to exhibit.

Granites are generally consistent in pattern. But I like the movement of marble patterning. If you plan to install a marble-slab countertop, ask the fabricator to show you the actual entire piece. That way, you won't end up as I did 10 years ago. I chose a countertop slab from a small marble sample. Later, with the countertop in place, I was shocked by drifts of color and markings on the entire piece.

Marble tiles are installed by the tile installer and sold by the box. Solid countertops, or slabs, come from an entirely different subcontractor, a stone fabricator, who buys his slabs from a stone yard. Stone tiles are subjected to many manufacturing processes that can alter their appearance radically. Stone slabs look essentially the same as when they were dug from the earth.

Grout: The Tie That Binds

While it's true that grout comes in many colors, my advice is that grout should never be colored. It's like purple contact lenses, which just look synthetic and odd. Grout should be *grout-colored*, which is not really just one color but a natural range from light gray-white to dark gray. The lighter the tile, the lighter the grout should be. Pure white grout on the floor is usually a mistake unless you plan to bleach it weekly. When white grout gets damp, it turns gray. In high-traffic areas, grout accumulates dirt and darkens, and you end up with track marks in the area in front of the toilet, sink, and tub. All-white grout is best left for wall and ceiling tile.

The more rustic your tile, the wider your grout lines should be. A machine-cut tile calls for a thin, even, consis-

"Pure white grout on the floor is usually a mistake unless you plan to bleach it weekly."

tent grout line. A rustic tile, such as terra-cotta or tumbled marble, takes a wider grout line that is less sharply defined because the edges of the tiles are not precise. When you shop, ask the salesperson how much grout he or she recommends for the tile you are buying.

TOILETS

When remodeling an existing bath, it's best to keep the fixtures, especially the toilet, in the same place. Toilets are attached to waste lines that are roughly the size of your thigh. You can move an existing toilet approximately 12 inches without disrupting function, but beyond that the gravitational pull that is necessary for an efficient flush will be compromised. In new construction, it's least expensive to keep waste lines and bathrooms back-to-back. If you are creating a new bathroom layout, try to find a place for the toilet that isn't in a direct line with the door.

Toilet Trends. The current rage is for "toilet rooms." I never had one and don't usually specify them, but a knee wall or a half wall is a much-desired and welcome addition. It's great for privacy, especially if the room will be shared. If you don't have the luxury of a layout that will permit a knee wall, try to tuck in the toilet near the side of the tub or beside the vanity.

Toilet bowls come in two sizes: standard and elongated. Elongated bowls are 2 inches longer than the standard types and are considered more comfortable and sanitary.

In a small bath, above, the toilet has to go wherever it will fit into the room. Larger layouts may afford space for a separate toilet room, right.

They're also more expensive. A two-piece toilet features a separate tank and bowl; a one-piece model is lower and sleeker in appearance. Before manufacturers improved on the *gravity-fed,* low-flush toilets that are now mandated, an interim solution was the *pressure-assisted* "airplane flush." Although it does a great job, it makes a heck of a loud noise. There are different toilet styles, as well. Some look contemporary, while others have traditional-style details. But rather than shopping for the "Charleston" or the "Rembrandt" model, look for a toilet that simply flushes efficiently and quietly.

Why Women Love Tubs

John Lennon once said that he knew why women had less stress than men: they take baths. For those of us who

prefer to shower, a bath is neither a daily routine nor a sacred ritual. But I concede that the moment I ease myself into a hot bath and make myself temporarily unavailable is the happiest time for me. And I am not alone. I recently read that Barbara Walters gets through boring evening events by reminding herself that in an hour she will be home in her hot bath. And Sandra Bullock says that on good days she takes two hot baths. Me, too. Also on bad days. Baths are restorative. The Japanese know that, and so did the ancient Romans.

Tub Size. Enjoying a great bath doesn't have to involve a sumptuous tub, either. In fact, if you think that an extra-long tub is best, guess what? It is bad for the back. For a healthy soak, your toes should be up against the foot of the tub giving you support and keeping you from slipping under water. Tubs really don't have to be more than 66 inches long, and even that may be too long for some people. For most, a standard 60-inch-long model will do.

Now, a *deeper* tub is wonderful for a full soak. Wider tubs (up to about 42 inches) are also great. Or how about some deck space or a built-in headrest at the end of the tub to lean on? If you're designing a tub deck, you could put the faucet on the far side of the tub so that you don't have to climb over it to get in and out. But if children or disabled family members will bathe here, it may

A roomy soaking tub, left, can be built into a custom surround. A telephone-style mixer, right, sits neatly on this tub's deck.

be safer to install the fittings so that they are easily accessible from inside and outside of the tub.

Tub Materials. Typically tubs are made of cast iron, enameled steel, fiberglass, or acrylic. The only disadvantage of cast iron is that it is cold, and the water has to heat the enamel surface. Cast-iron tubs are also heavy, so you have to have a solid floor to support them.

Enameled-steel tubs sound tinny if you tap them, and the coating chips easily. However, they are less expensive and lighter in weight than cast iron. Fiberglass, as I learned

when I stayed at my friend Nancy's house, scratches easily and sounds hollow if you tap on it. Instead of taking her bath mats outside to shake them out, I lazily shook them into Nancy's tub with the intention of then vacuuming the tub. I used the brush attachment, but still the tub

THE TRUTH ABOUT GLASS DOORS

Sometimes when people are freshening up their bathrooms, they think that the best thing they can do is put glass doors on a combined shower and tub. I hate them. Okay, if you have three adolescent sons who shower for hours on end, then it might be worth it to help keep the water in the tub. But I think taking a bath behind these glass doors, which only open halfway, is just too confining. What's more, you can never sit on the edge of the tub or rest a magazine or a glass on it. Plus, the track makes it uncomfortable to lean over the tub's edge to bathe a child.

When my clients and I talk about decorating baths with glass doors, everyone always wants to know how to hide them. If you drape the doors with oodles of fabric, you'll soon have moldy, damp, dank fabric.

Of course, if your tub is in the "extra" bathroom, and the shower gets little use, drape and swag the curtain like crazy. But, if you shower frequently, choose a water-repellent cotton curtain that stays fresh longer and can be washed regularly.

scratched terribly. I ended up huffing and puffing and buffing the scratches, which were only superficial. However, a fiberglass tub is economical and, like an enameled-steel tub, lightweight.

Acrylic tubs are reinforced with fiberglass, so they are sturdier while remaining lightweight. A good-quality one will cost about as much as a low-end cast-iron tub.

Beyond the typical, tubs can be made of anything and everything: glass block, mosaic tile, marble, stone, even wood. If you choose any of these, however, you had better have the best and most competent installer on the planet—and a good-size wallet!

Whirlpools. One upgrade, the whirlpool tub, adds convenience and comfort. It's a good investment. A whirlpool (or jetted) tub has become a standard in the master bath. If you're debating about whether to install a whirlpool tub, it will add resale value to your house. The smaller size, which is approximately 66 x 38 inches, works for one person, but larger models can accommodate two or more people. There are a few things to consider about the whirlpool you choose. First, can your bathroom floor support the weight? You'll need at least 50 gallons of water for a satisfying soak—even more if it's a large tub. Also, keep in mind that you have to install a 50- to 60-gallon water heater, if you don't already own one. What optional features will you select? How many jets: three, four, six, ten? Do you want an in-line heater? A special color or shape? Variable-speed pumps? All of these things are tempting, but they will boost the price.

Fairer Fittings

Put bathtub faucets where you can reach them to adjust temperature and flow without getting into the tub. If your faucet is deck mounted, meaning it is installed in a tub-surround and doesn't come out from the wall, consider the length of the spout. It has to be long enough to reach well into the tub. A hand-held sprayer, in addition to a traditional spout, is a wonderful amenity. This is great for rinsing the tub, washing your hair, and bathing children. I had one in my last house, and I really miss it. Sometimes it's referred to as a telephone-style mixer because one version resembles an old-fashioned telephone receiver as it rests in a cradle above the faucet handles and spout. It can also sit in a ring that's mounted on the wall.

I'll bet you didn't know that you can also use an umbrella in the bathtub. An "umbrella" is an apparatus that hangs from the ceiling to create a shower in a tub that didn't previously have one. I had one in my first house and installed one in this house in my daughter's bath. Be sure to use several shower curtains with it to completely

surround the tub and keep water from spraying all over the floor.

A charming umbrella shower can be retrofitted for use with a vintage bathtub.

Faucet Materials. These can include chrome, colored enamel, nickel, pewter, brass, ceramic, gold-plate, gold, or a combination of these. Finishes can also be polished or brushed, or can feature inserts of crystal or stone. Your budget and your taste will determine what you choose. Style is available at all price points, but quality is not. Even

"One upgrade, the whirlpool tub, adds convenience and comfort."

Faucets come in a variety of styles — from single lever to cross handles — in both matte and shiny finishes.

mid-priced sets come with technologically advanced finishes that keep them looking new longer. It used to be that tiny holes in the lacquer coating on brass allowed air and moisture to penetrate the finish and cause pitting. Today, some brass fittings come with a lifetime warranty on the finish, so you won't encounter that problem.

In my experience, I have found that men generally like faucets with levers, and women like handles with spokes. Men like to be able to turn the water off with their elbow. I guess that's convenient when their hands are covered with shaving cream. Levers are easier to use because you don't have to grab them, but handles can be quite decorative.

If you're looking for an inexpensive updated look for your faucets, you can sometimes retain the existing valves but replace the handles. Some manufacturers are even designing new interchangeable faucet handles today. Another client, Lou, had old faucet handles with missing "lids." I was going to try to fabricate a replacement because I didn't want to go to the expense of buying a new lavatory set. The carpenter told me I could just get new handles. We not only saved money but also gave the bathroom fittings an updated look.

Looks are important, but the really essential aspect of a faucet is its inner parts. For a reliable unit, choose one with high-quality ceramic-disk valves. Plastic-disk valves, which is what you get with a cheap faucet, won't last. You can buy a good faucet for just a couple of hundred dollars. It will save you money in repairs over the long run.

SHOWER POWER

These days, everyone seems to prefer a shower with a glass enclosure. I don't get it. For the most part, I close my eyes in the shower. Why would I want a view? More puzzling, why would I want anyone to view me? Even if you want a view, the glass steams up the minute you turn the water on. I think people believe a glass shower makes the room look bigger. I disagree. I think the shower just looks like a room within a room. Besides, who wants to look at your shower brush, shampoo, and washcloth? What's more, glass is expensive.

Shower Door. Glass shower doors come in two varieties: Chevy and Rolls Royce. The latter is seamless. Models range in cost from about $500 to many times that amount. I think a simple, shatterproof shower door, either chrome-framed or frameless, is a perfect choice. It does not have to be oversized. I have a 22-inch shower door, and it works just fine. Although some experts recommend a shower door that opens into the room, I prefer one that opens into the shower. That way, water that collects on the inside of the door will run into the shower instead of onto the bathroom floor when you exit, creating a potential hazard.

A hand sprayer can accommodate kids and adults alike.

Picking Up Steam and Other Amenities

Steam showers and jetted showers are popular, but if you surface a steam shower in marble or stone, you will have to double the steam generator capacity. Why? Because stone is 15 degrees cooler than anything around it. If you've been wondering why your steam shower doesn't seem to heat up, maybe this is why. And if your shower will include massaging jets, you may need to boost the size of your water heater as well.

Shower Heads. Shower heads come in many sizes and shapes. They can be fixed or handheld. Some shower heads come with pulsating sprays and adjustable speeds and intensities. You can experience everything from a gentle mist to an invigorating deluge. When the shower will be used by several members of the household, it's a good idea to provide a shower head that is adjustable to various heights, as well. Some people mount several spray jets on opposite sides of the shower wall for a soothing hydromassage. But I'll cut to the chase and just tell you: if you're interested in something basic, get a shower head with a wonderful strong spray and good adjustable spray control.

Beyond the basic, there are other types to consider. A *rain dome* is an oversize shower head mounted on the ceiling that drenches you with water. Men love them; women don't. With a rain dome, your hair is always going to get 100 percent wet. They are a good idea *in addition* to a wall-mounted shower head. If you want your hair to remain dry, be sure the rain dome is turned off. A *rain bar* is another enticing option. This vertical bar with many small openings is mounted on the shower wall and gives the effect of a fine rain.

Open Bench

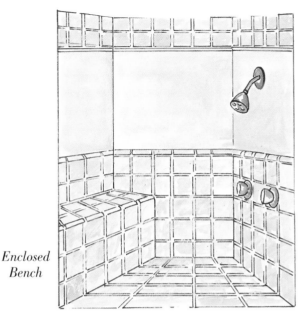

Enclosed Bench

Whether you have a Rolls Royce or a Chevy shower, always remember to place the shower controls where you have easy access to them and where you are able to adjust the water temperature and spray without having to step or lean into the shower and under the water.

Sitting Pretty. A bench is one of the best amenities you can add to a shower. I designed my first bench at the request of a customer. A seat or bench in the shower, along with its own handheld spray, is the ultimate in convenience and safety. If you build a bench, make sure the front panel is solid all the way to the floor. Cleaning under an open shower bench is inconvenient.

Cutting Clutter. Built-in niches are wonderful, and you should specify them if you are adding a new

A built-in storage niche can hold soap and shampoo.

" . . .the exact same bowl can cost $175 or $475, depending on the brand name. "

shower. But don't put them in the wall directly opposite the door. No matter how expensive your rinses and creams, an array of plastic bottles can make even the most elegant shower look messy. If you are building a niche into your new shower, be sure it tilts slightly forward so that water — and germs and mildew — don't collect in it. If you can't have a built-in shower niche, install a screw-in wire basket or shower caddy to keep everything handy and off the floor.

SINKS

Like everything else, bathrooms are not immune to fads. A bathroom fashion I find alarming is the above-counter sink. This sink resembles a bowl sitting on a lowered countertop. Not only do I think it looks ridiculous, but I don't think it's comfortable to use either.

Sink Types. I like the look of a pedestal sink; it's like a beautiful piece of sculpture. For a powder room, I am a pedestal-sink advocate. I replaced my powder room's original built-in sink and awkward vanity with a pedestal sink because of the tight configuration of the space. The vanity projected clumsily in front of the door. Although I sacrificed storage, I love the way the room looks now.

Vanity sinks can be surface mounted (also called drop-in, overmounted, or self-rimming sinks) or undermounted, which means that the bowl is attached underneath the countertop. An integral sink combines the countertop material and the bowl (typically stone or a solid-surface laminate) in one seamless piece. I learned my sink lessons from Dr. Roger Duvivier, a noted obstetrician who specializes in high-risk cases. We're talking sterile here. He could not abide the scum that collected around the rim of his surface-mounted sink. We quickly replaced it with an integral design. With one sweep of the sponge, the countertop and sink are clean.

When buying a sink, don't be fooled by brands. A lot of the high-end bath suppliers buy the same standard porcelain bowls used by mass market, lower-end suppliers. Therefore, the exact same bowl can cost $175 or $475, depending on the brand name. I recommend spending your money on something unique and truly special — not on a name. Also, buy your sink and faucet set at the same time. For one client, Ann, I got a charming small sink for her playroom bath with an equally charming small faucet set. The problem was that the

A self-rimming sink has to be sealed around the edge.

An **undermounted sink** can keep dirt and germs off the countertop.

VENTILATION

Finally, this isn't the most glamorous aspect of a bath makeover, but it's an important one. Stagnant air and mildew in the bathroom are unhealthy and can ruin your decorating efforts. The proper fan will eliminate odors and damaging moisture. It should be included in any bath renovation plan. Put the fan on a switch that is separate from the lights. When the fan and light are operated from the same switch, every time you need the light, you'll have the roar of the fan. That's not something you want in the middle of the night. I also suggest installing the fan low to the ground, either under the sink or near the toilet. I hate ceilings that are marked with lighting fixtures and fan covers. A low-to-the-floor fan works just fine in the powder room unless there is a shower.

"I also suggest installing the fan low to the ground, either under the sink or near the toilet."

faucet did not project out enough into the sink bowl, and it was impossible to insert a glass or your hands under the faucet for a splash or a sip. This was completely impractical. The sink and the faucet must be compatible and in proportion to each other.

Windows that open and close easily—plus an exhaust fan— are important for bathroom ventilation.

GLOSSARY

Accent Lighting: A type of lighting that highlights an area or object to emphasize that aspect of a room's character.

Ambient Lighting: General illumination that surrounds a room. There is no visible source of the light.

Backsplash: The vertical part at the rear and sides of a countertop that protects the adjacent wall.

Built-In: Any element, such as a bookcase or cabinetry, that is built into a wall or an existing frame.

Case Good: A piece of furniture used for storage, including cabinets, dressers, and desks.

Code: A locally or nationally enforced mandate regarding structural design, materials, plumbing, or electrical systems that state what you can or cannot do when you build or remodel. Codes are intended to protect standards of health, safety, and land use.

Color Wheel: A pie-shaped diagram showing the range and relationships of pigment and dye colors. Three equidistant wedge-shaped slices are the primaries; in between are the secondary and tertiary colors into which the primaries combine. Though represented as discrete slices, the hues form a continuum.

Dimmer Switch: A switch that can vary the intensity of the light it controls.

Distressed Finish: A decorative paint technique in which the final paint coat is sanded and battered to produce an aged appearance.

Fittings: The plumbing devices that bring water to the fixtures. These can include faucets, spouts, and drains.

Fluorescent Lighting: A glass tube coated on the interior with phosphor, a chemical compound that emits light when activated by ultraviolet energy. Air in the tube is replaced with a combination of argon gas and a small amount of mercury.

Focal Point: The dominant element in a room or design, usually the first to catch your eye.

Framed Cabinet: A cabinet with a full frame across the face of the cabinet box.

Frameless Cabinet: A cabinet without a face frame. It may also be called a "European-style" cabinet.

Frieze: A horizontal band at the top of the wall or just below the cornice.

Hardware: Wood, plastic, or metal-plated trim found on the exterior of furniture, such as knobs, handles, and decorative trim.

Incandescent Lighting: A bulb (lamp) that converts electric power into light by passing electric current through a filament of tungsten wire.

Molding: An architectural band that can either trim a line where materials join or create a linear decoration. It is typically made of wood, but metal, plaster, or polymer (plastic) is also used.

Mortise-and-Tenon Joinery: A hole (mortise) cut into a piece of wood that receives a projecting piece (tenon) to create a joint. It is often used in fine furniture making.

Pattern Matching: To align a repeating pattern when joining together two pieces of fabric or wallpaper.

Task Lighting: Lighting that concentrates in specific areas for tasks, such as preparing food, applying makeup, reading, or doing crafts.

Tufting: The fabric of an upholstered piece or a mattress that is drawn tightly to secure the padding, creating regularly spaced indentations.

Uplight: Also used to describe the lights themselves, this is actually the term for light that is directed upward toward the ceiling or the upper part of walls.

Welt: A cord, often covered by fabric, that is used as an elegant trim on cushions, slipcovers, etc.

Work Triangle: The area bounded by the lines that connect the sink, range, and refrigerator.

PHOTO CREDITS*

Cover: *Photography:* George Ross **pp. 1, 2, 6, 8** *Photography:* George Ross. **p. 10** *Photography:* George Ross. **p. 11** *Photography (clockwise from top right):* Courtesy of Motif Designs, Courtesy of Motif Designs, George Ross, George Ross. **pp. 12, 15–16, 19** *Photography:* Courtesy of Motif Designs.* **p. 20** *Photography:* George Ross. **p. 21** *Photography:* George Ross. **pp. 22–23** *Photography:* Courtesy of Motif Designs. **p. 25** *Photography:* Mark Lohman; *Designer:* Janet Lohman. **p. 27** *Photography:* Mark Lohman. **pp. 28, 30** *Photography:* George Ross. **p. 32** *Photography:* Courtesy of Motif Designs. **p. 33** *Photography (top right):* George Ross. *Photography (swatches):* Christine Elasigue. **p. 34** *Photography:* Christine Elasigue. **p. 35** *Photography:* Mark Lohman. **pp. 36, 39** *Photography:* George Ross. **p. 40** *Photography:* Mark Lohman. **p. 41** *Photography:* Christine Elasigue. **pp. 42–43** *Photography:* Courtesy of Motif Designs. **p. 45** *Photography (left):* Lilo Raymond. *Photography (swatches):* Christine Elasigue. **p. 46** *Photography:* Courtesy of Motif Designs. **p. 48** *Photography (left):* George Ross. *Photography (swatches):* Christine Elasigue. **p. 49** *Photography:* George Ross. **p. 50** *Photography:* Christine Elasigue. **p. 51** *Photography:* George Ross. **p. 52** *Photography:* Christine Elasigue. **p. 53** *Photography:* Mark Lohman. **p. 54** *Photography (left):* Rob Melnychuk; *Designer:* Wendy Williams Watt. *Photography (top right):* Tria Giovan. *Photography (swatches):* Christine Elasigue. **pp. 56, 58–61** *Photography:* Courtesy of Motif Designs. **pp. 62–63** *Photography:* George Ross. **pp. 64–66, 68–70, 72–77, 79–81** *Photography:* Courtesy of Motif Designs. **p. 82** *Photography (swatch, top left):* Christine Elasigue; *Photography (top right, bottom left):* Courtesy of Motif Designs. **p. 83** *Photography:* Courtesy of Motif Designs. **p. 84** *Photography:* davidduncanlivingston.com. **p. 86** *Photography:* George Ross. **pp. 89–90** *Photography:* Courtesy of Motif Designs. **p. 91** *Photography:* davidduncanlivingston.com. **pp. 92, 95, 97** *Photography:*

Courtesy of Motif Designs. **p. 98** *Photography:* Melabee M Miller; *Designer:* Suzanne S. Curtis, ASID. **pp. 103–104** *Photography:* Courtesy of Motif Designs. **p. 109** *Photography:* davidduncanlivingston.com. **p. 110** *Photography:* davidduncanlivingston.com. **pp. 111–112** *Photography:* Courtesy of Motif Designs. **p. 113** *Photography:* davidduncanlivingston.com. **pp. 119–121** *Photography:* Courtesy of Motif Designs. **p. 122** *Photography:* George Ross. **p. 124** *Photography:* davidduncanlivingston.com. **p. 125** *Photography:* George Ross. **p. 127** *Photography (top):* Courtesy of Motif Designs; *Photography (bottom):* davidduncanlivingston.com. **p. 127** *Photography:* Mark Lohman. **p. 128** *Photography:* Courtesy of Motif Designs. **p. 130** *Photography:* Mark Lohman. **p. 131** *Photography:* Courtesy of Motif Designs. **p. 132** *Photography:* davidduncanlivingston.com. **p. 133** *Photography:* Courtesy of Motif Designs. **p. 135** *Photography (top):* George Ross; *Photography (bottom):* davidduncanlivingston.com. **p. 136** *Photography:* Courtesy of Motif Designs. **p. 137** *Photography:* Courtesy of Motif Designs. **p. 138** *Photography:* George Ross. **p. 139** *Photography:* Courtesy of Motif Designs. **p. 141** *Photography:* Courtesy of Motif Designs. **p. 142** *Photography:* George Ross. **p.143** *Photography:* Courtesy of Motif Designs. **pp. 144–147** *Photography:* George Ross. **p. 148** Courtesy of Motif Designs. **p. 150** *Photography:* George Ross. **p. 151** *Photography:* Courtesy of Motif Designs. **p. 152** *Photography:* George Ross. **p. 154** *Photography:* davidduncanlivingston.com. **p. 155** *Photography:* Courtesy of Motif Designs. **p. 156** *Photography:* George Ross. **p. 157** *Photography:* davidduncanlivingston.com. **p. 158** *Photography:* George Ross. **p. 159** *Photography:* Anne Gummerson. **pp. 161, 163** *Photography:* davidduncanlivingston.com. **p. 164** *Photography:* Courtesy of Motif Designs. **p. 165** *Photography:* Mark Lohman. **pp. 166–169** *Photography:* davidduncanlivingston.com. **p. 170** *Photography:* Courtesy of Motif Designs.

p. 171 *Photography:* George Ross. **pp. 172–173** *Photography:* davidduncanlivingston.com. **p. 174** *Photography:* Mark Samu. **pp. 176–177** *Photography:* davidduncanlivingston.com. **pp. 178, 180** *Photography:* George Ross. **pp. 181–182** *Photography:* Courtesy of Motif Designs. **pp. 183–184** *Photography:* Peter Tata. **p. 185** *Photography:* Mark Samu. **p. 187** *Photography:* Courtesy of Motif Designs. **p. 188** *Photography:* Mark Samu. **pp. 190–191** *Photography:* Mark Lohman. **p. 193** *Photography:* Anne Gummerson. **pp. 194, 197** *Photography:* George Ross. **p. 198** *Photography:* Mark Samu; *Designer:* Bob Altavilla. **p. 201** *Photography:* Mark Lohman; *Designer:* Kitty Bartholomew. **pp. 202–203** *Photography:* Mark Lohman. **p. 204** *Photography:* Mark Lohman; *Designer:* Darren Hinault. **p. 205** *Photography:* Mark Samu; *Designer:* Langsam Robin. **pp. 206–208** *Photography:* Mark Lohman; *Designer:* Rick Berman. **p. 210** *Photography (top):* Mark Samu. *Photography (bottom):* Courtesy of Motif Designs. **p. 211** *Photography:* Mark Lohman; *Designer:* Rick Berman. **p. 213** *Photography:* Mark Lohman. **p. 214** *Photography:* Mark Lohman; *Designer:* Janet Lohman. **pp. 216, 218, 219–21** *Photography:* George Ross. **p. 222** *Photography:* Mark Lohman. **p. 223** *Photography:* Mark Lohman. **p. 227** *Photography:* Anne Gummerson. **p. 228** *Photography:* Courtesy of Brawer & Hauptman Architects, Philadelphia, PA. **p. 229** *Photography:* George Ross. **p. 230** *Photography:* Courtesy of Brawer & Hauptman Architects, Philadelphia, PA. **p. 231** *Photography:* Anne Gummerson. **p. 232** *Photography (left):* Mark Lohman; *Designer:* Joe Ruggiero. *Photography (right):* Anne Gummerson. **p. 235** *Photography:* Mark Lohman; *Designer:* Kathryne Dahlman. **p. 236** *Photography:* George Ross. **p. 237** *Photography:* George Ross. **p. 238** *Photography:* Mark Lohman; *Designer:* Barclay Butera. **p. 239** *Photography:* Mark Lohman; *Designer:* Barclay Butera. **p. 240** *Photography:* George Ross. **p. 241** *Photography:* Mark Lohman; *Designer:* Cross Interiors.

p. 243 *Photography:* George Ross. **p. 245** *Photography:* George Ross. **p. 246** *Photography:* Mark Lohman; *Designer:* Joe Ruggiero. **p. 247** *Photography:* Mark Samu. **p. 248** *Photography:* davidduncanlivingston.com. **p. 250** *Photography:* George Ross. **p. 252** *Photography (top):* Mark Lohman; *Designer:* Cross Interiors. *Photography (bottom):* Mark Lohman. **p. 253** *Photography:* Mark Lohman. **pp. 254-255** *Photography:* Mark Lohman; *Designer:* Cross Interiors. **p. 256** *Photography:* Mark Lohman. **p. 257** *Photography:* George Ross. **p. 259** *Photography:* Andrew McKinney; *Designer:* LouAnn Bauer. **p. 261** *Photography:* Mark Lohman. **pp. 262, 264–265** *Photography:* George Ross. **pp. 268–269** *Photography:* Courtesy of Motif Designs. **pp. 271–272** *Photography:* Mark Lohman; *Designer:* Lynn Pries. **p. 273** *Photography:* Courtesy of Motif Designs. **pp. 274–275, 277–278** *Photography:* Mark Lohman. **p. 279** *Photography:* George Ross. **p. 280** *Photography:* Courtesy of Motif Designs. **p. 282** *Photography:* George Ross. **p. 283** *Photography:* Mark Lohman. **p. 284** *Photography:* Mark Lohman. **p. 285** *Photography:* Anne Gummerson. **p. 287** *Photography:* Mark Lohman. **p. 288** *Photography (bottom left):* Anne Gummerson; *Photography:* Courtesy of Motif Designs. **pp. 290–291** *Photography:* George Ross. **pp. 293–295** *Photography:* Courtesy of Motif Designs. **p. 302** *Photography:* George Ross.

*All photographs from Motif Designs and by George Ross, *Designer:* Lyn Peterson.

Most fabrics and wallcoverings featured in this book are by Motif Designs, (800) 431-2424.

INDEX

INDEX (CONTINUED)

Lyn's 15 Favorit

1. **CUTLERY DRAWER INSERT.** Hire a carpenter to make a special insert for the drawer where you store your silver cutlery and serving pieces. Line it with Pacific cloth, which is the feltlike material that keeps your silver from tarnishing. I just did this for my 200-year-old French buffet. I was tired of heaving my heavy silverware box in and out of the lower cabinet where I kept it. Now I don't have to. The made-to-measure insert is designed to minute specifications, and it simply drops into a drawer in the buffet. Not only is my silverware more accessible, but I am able to neatly store my tiny demitasse spoons as well as my tall and narrow salad utensils in their own perfectly proportioned compartments. I maximized my storage and made my silverware more accessible at the same time. Cost for my most extravagant drawer (12 compartments): $175.

2. **DIMMER SWITCH.** Create "instant atmosphere." Buy a $6 dimmer switch at the hardware store and install it yourself, if you're comfortable with that, or hire an electrician. It's not a big job, and it's not expensive. I was at a client's home and we were arguing over whether to put lightbulbs measuring 40 watts (pleasing light) or 75 watts (reading light) in their family room wall sconces. What a debate! Sure you can do three-way bulbs, but inevitably the setting you use the most burns out first and you end up with one that's too bright or too dark. With a dimmer switch, you have almost infinite degrees of light at your fingertips.

3. **SWIVELS AND CASTORS.** One of my most appreciated decorator tricks is a swivel, or castors, which I retrofit to an existing upholstered chair. In my own home, we added a rock swivel to a curbside find that is now the most sought-after seat in the house. When I brought it home atop the baby carriage, my husband cried, "That's junk!" I told him that when this old chair was constructed, "they didn't make 'junk' back then." The treasured chair is positioned in our breakfast room between the eating area and the small TV. The kids love it so much, we had to apply a five-minute-limit rule on it so that everyone can take a turn.

4. **ARM TO A SIDE.** What happens when your family outgrows the dining table and chairs you bought for your first home or apartment? You can add leaves to make the table larger (hiring a carpenter to make them, if necessary) but what about extra seating? In many cases, I have taken a dining room's existing armchairs and converted them to side chairs. All you have to do is remove the arms and touch up the finish. At a local wood-stripping shop, this costs me about $100 a chair, which is a lot less than the price of a new chair. Then I use tall upholstered chairs (wing chairs, for example) to replace the host and hostess seating pieces.

5. **SHOP AT HOME.** Our homes get too set. We put a piece of furniture, a picture, or some accessory in place, and there it remains until death do us part or until we replace it. But I like to shop at home, and by that I mean: when I'm tired of the way a room looks, I don't run out and buy all new furnishings. Instead, I like to move things around to other places or rooms in the house. No one does this better than my friend, Kristiina, although it can be exhausting. Her library table moves to the entry; then a year later it goes out to the porch. The loveseat in her bedroom winds up in a reading alcove on the children's upstairs landing. What was over the mantel is now under the bed. It doesn't always work, and sometimes after a day or so, things go right back to where they were. But when it does work, nothing is more gratifying. Things look fresh and new, and no one spends any money—oh well, maybe a little. After all, you have to replace the loveseat from the bedroom with something.

6. **KEEP A STRICT ROTATION.** When my mother's friend, Kay McMahon, died, she left the most beautiful old rugs behind. Unfortunately, they were worn in one corner. Wear is charming but only when it is more or less evenly distributed. Rotate your rugs, cushions, mattresses, even the curtain panels. In my house we tend to sit on one section of the sectional. If I did not rotate my cushions regularly, I would end up with wear and tear on the one flank and pristine perfection on the other. As to curtains, the way sun enters my rooms, only one side of my curtains is exposed to fading rays. By rotating the panels regularly, I extend the life of my curtains by distributing the wear evenly.

7. **HOUSE FILE.** Keep a hanging file that contains a record of the yardage requirements for fabrics, carpets, and wallpaper. That way when you want to redecorate, you will have some of the vital information at hand. Also file away sales receipts for purchases, especially antiques, which get more valuable with time. Include the names, company names, and phone numbers of all tradespeople you regularly use: mason, roofer, etc. That way when you need one, you won't get lost looking through the phone book thinking, "His name was Mario, but what was his business called?"

Real Life Ideas

8. **STORAGE SOLUTION.** I was lamenting that I was of an age when I had so much stuff that storage was a problem when my wise friend, Kristiina, said that the issue was really organization. It's not about putting things away, but about having them accessible and using them. How true. Now my good silver is at my fingertips, and I use it often.

9. **PARTY LIGHTING.** When having a party, put a light on in all the rooms in the house, including the attic. Not a bright light, but a little warm glow. Your house will look larger and more welcoming to your guests. In fact, it's my philosophy that if your house looks good during the day, you can thank the site, the climate, or the architect. If your house looks bad at night, you have no one to blame but yourself. It's all electric. Just plug it in.

10. **VERSATILE OTTOMANS.** Ottomans can be store-bought, or you can buy the legs and make one to your size. Any upholsterer can do it, and legs are available through hardware stores, the upholsterer, or home centers. Styles range from fluted, turned, tapered to simple brass balls. If you don't want a visible leg, then just go straight to the upholsterer with the size you need. Some people use a large ottoman as a coffee table. If you don't, you may need a place to store it when it's not in use. Tuck it under a side table or under the arm of your seating, or even under the coffee table if you can.

11. **COFFEE TABLES.** I like a high coffee table. I think the proportion is better, and it works as a footrest and a workable, usable surface. An upright tea table is best if you want something antique, or have the legs of an old dining table, side table, or work surface cut down. Keep the removed portions and use them for something else, such as legs for a custom-made ottoman. When deciding on the size and placement of your coffee table, make it reachable from the seating.

12. **ENTRY HALLWAY.** This is where the first and last impressions of your home are made. Install a new hanging light fixture. Sconces are always nice. Hang a mirror on the wall. Get a decorative shelf for under the mirror that has a place for a seasonal accessory that you can change, but also have a key tray and a place to put your gloves. Paint the walls a deeper color than your living area, and buy a small area rug in complementary colors to make this space memorable.

13. **QUICK CHANGE FOR A ROOM.** Install a chair rail. Usually a chair rail looks best when it's 32 inches from the floor and stained or painted to match the rest of the woodwork in the room. Paint the new wainscoted area a slightly deeper shade than the upper portion of the wall, or hang wallpaper. Dining rooms, dens, and entry halls all seem to benefit from this treatment.

14. **COLLECTIONS.** Dig into that box of stuff from grandma, and do something with your finds: dance cards, hatpins, old eyeglasses. Take the things you like to collect — crystals, rocks, or napkin rings for example — and find an original way to display them. Arrange them in memory boxes, and hang them at eye level on the wall.

15. **PRESHRUNK FABRIC.** When fabricating anything, prewash the cloth before you sew. Most fabrics shrink the first time you wash them. That way, when you launder your linen curtains or wash your sectional seat covers, they won't be too short or too small. Sure you can have them dry-cleaned, but is that ever really clean? Besides, it's expensive to dry-clean them regularly. Wash these things at home; the cost is pennies.

10 little things that mean a lot

1. Bright white ceiling paint

2. A four-seater sofa

3. Strong paint color for small spaces

4. Oiled brass hardware, which ages handsomely with time and use

5. Gardener's moss applied to plastic pots and lanky stems

6. Lots of cashmere, camel's hair, or lamb's wool throws

7. Washable everyday cotton napkins

8. Creamy mix-and-match Wedgwood china

9. Children's art displayed prominently

10. Bedspreads, not comforters

Have a home decorating, improvement, or gardening project? Look for these and other fine **Creative Homeowner books** wherever books are sold. . .

Design advice and industry tips for choosing window treatments. Over 225 illustrations. 176 pp.; 9"×10"
BOOK # 279431

How to work with space, color, pattern, texture. Over 300 photos. 256 pp.; 9"×10"
BOOK #: 279667

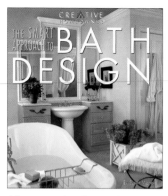

All you need to know about designing a bath. Over 150 color photos. 176 pp.; 9"×10"
BOOK #: 287225

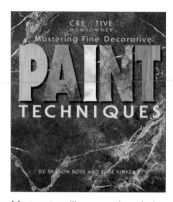

Master stenciling, sponging, glazing, marbling, and more. Over 300 illustrations. 272 pp.; 9"×10"
BOOK #: 279550

Projects to personalize your rooms with paint and paper. 300 color photos. 176 pp.; 9"×10"
BOOK #: 279723

Learn how to make the most of color. More than 150 color photos. 176 pp.; 9"×10"
BOOK #: 287264

Original ideas for decorating and organizing kids' rooms. Over 200 color photos. 176 pp.; 9"×10"
BOOK #: 279473

Advice for choosing tile for interior and exterior decorating projects. Over 250 photos. 176 pp.; 9"×10"
BOOK #: 279824

Complete houseplant guide. 200 readily available plants; more than 400 photos. 192 pp.; 9"×10"
BOOK #: 275243

Create beautiful, healthier, lower-maintenance lawns. Over 300 illustrations. 160 pp.; 9"×10"
BOOK #: 274359

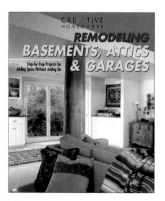

How to convert unused space into useful living area. 570 illustrations. 192 pp.; 8¹/₂"×10⁷/₈"
BOOK #: 277680

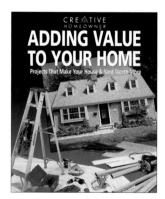

Filled with DIY projects to repair, upgrade, and add value. 500 illustrations. 176 pp.; 8¹/₂"×10⁷/₈"
BOOK #: 277006

For more information, and to order direct, call 800-631-7795; in New Jersey, 201-934-7100.
Please visit our Web site at www.creativehomeowner.com